Lenin

Life and
Times

Lenin
Seán Sheehan

HAUS PUBLISHING • LONDON

First published in Great Britain in 2010 by
Haus Publishing Ltd
70 Cadogan Place
London SW1X 9AH
www.hauspublishing.com

Copyright © Seán Sheehan, 2009

The moral right of the author has been asserted

A CIP catalogue record for this book
is available from the British Library

ISBN 978-1-905791-26-2

Typeset in Sabon by MacGuru Ltd
Printed and bound by CPI Antony Rowe, Chippenham
Front cover: Getty Images

Contents

The Ulyanov family *circa* 1881. (Left to right: seated) Maria Alexandrovna (mother) with Maria; Dimitri; Ilya Nikolaievich (father); Vladimir (Lenin). (Standing) Olga; Alexander; Anna.

The Boy from the Volga

The vast Russian Empire stretched 5,000 miles from its Polish territory in the west to Vladivostok and the Sea of Japan in the east, and from the Arctic Ocean in the north to a border with Afghanistan in the south. It had been in existence for over 250 years when, on 10 April 1870, one more of its imperial subjects was born in the town of Simbirsk (Ulyanovsk) on the banks of the Volga. The date could be said to mark the beginning of the empire's end and the start of something new in human history. It would be recalled 75 years later, when the Red Army's final assault on Nazi Germany was being planned. It suggested itself as auspicious and the date was chosen for the appointed day when Berlin would fall to Soviet forces.[1]

In 1870, Simbirsk was famous for very little and the town was not yet connected by railway with the capital St Petersburg, a thousand miles to the north-west. The town's river, when it was not frozen over, was the major means of transport. The Volga, the longest river in Europe, flowed south into the Caspian Sea and the wooden houses of Simbirsk extended for miles along its high banks. Apart from a vodka distillery, a brewery and a candle factory there was little industrial development around the town; people made a living from the river and markets served the peasants from the surrounding countryside. A backwater in some respects, Simbirsk was nonetheless the capital town of Simbirsk province and, with a population approaching 40,000, possessed two good secondary schools, and had a substantial army garrison under the command of the province's governor.[2] Should the governor require it, physical force was at hand to quell any disorder that might break out in the area. The spiritual power of the Russian Empire, entrusted to the Russian Orthodox Church, was represented by the town's grand cathedral and it was here that the baby born on 10 April was christened Vladimir Ilyich Ulyanov. Had the priest known he was baptising Lenin he might have spared the holy water or, hoping for a divine intervention in the course of history, been more liberal in sprinkling it about.

The name Lenin, though, was one of the very many pseudonyms yet to be adopted by Vladimir Ilyich and the infant blessed in church was the child of a highly respectable middle-class couple who had newly moved to the town. The father, Ilya Ulyanov, had recently been appointed a school inspector for the province and when he took up his new post there were already two children in his family. Anna had been born in 1864, Alexander two years later, and his wife Maria Alexandrovna was again pregnant when they moved into rented accommodation in Simbirsk towards the end of 1869.

The family backgrounds of Ilya and Maria are complex but intriguing and, while Vladimir and his siblings shared a very conventional upbringing, there is an adventurous blending of ethnic and cultural factors in their kinship. The family history of Vladimir's mother is the more intricate of the two. Maria Alexandrovna Blank, born in St Petersburg in 1835, was brought up as a Protestant Lutheran by her mother who was of mixed German and Swedish ancestry.[3] Maria's father, Alexander Blank, was also a Christian but a Russian Orthodox one and, strictly speaking, his wife should have adopted his faith and brought up their children accordingly. Alexander, though, coming from a Jewish family, may not have felt strongly about the rival claims of different Christian sects. He was born as Srul (the Yiddish form of Israel) but had converted to Christianity in 1820 and adopted a new name. He had been educated in a non-Jewish state school, along with his brother Abel, who also became a Christian and took the name Dmitri, and the brothers went on to study medicine in St Petersburg and qualify as doctors. Their father, Moshko Blank, also renounced his Jewish identity and became a Christian after the death of his wife and it is very possible that all three of them did so in order to avoid Russian anti-Semitism.

It was in St Petersburg that Alexander Blank married but nine years later, when their daughter Maria was three, his wife died and he began to live with one of her sisters. This sister, whom he could not legally marry, was Yekaterina von Essen and her wealth, which came from her deceased husband, enabled them to purchase an estate and live a comfortable existence. Lenin's mother spent part of her

The partition of Poland that had begun in 1773 made eastern Poland part of the Russian Empire and led to the Pale of Settlement, beyond which Jews could only live by special licence. Although this was not always strictly enforced, for there were Jewish communities in St Petersburg and other cities, there were anti-Semitic regulations and prejudices that made life difficult for Jews seeking economic and social advancement outside of the Pale. Eight years after Lenin's death, his older sister Anna unearthed their family's Jewish background and wrote to Stalin to suggest that this information could be used to combat anti-Semitism – his response was firmly negative and Lenin's Jewish ancestry remained unknown.

Lenin's Family Tree

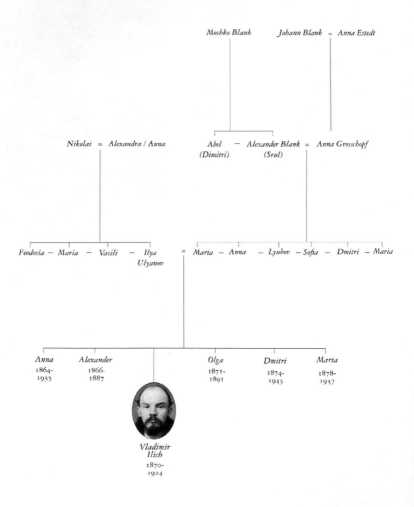

Moshko Blank   Johann Blank = Anna Estedt

Nikolai = Alexandra / Anna

Abel — Alexander Blank = Anna Grosschopf
(Dimitri)   (Srul)

Feodosia — Maria — Vasili — Ilya = Maria — Anna — Lyubov — Sofia — Dmitri — Maria
Ulyanov

Anna
1864-
1935

Alexander
1866-
1887

Olga
1871-
1891

Dmitri
1874-
1943

Maria
1878-
1937

Vladimir
Ilich
1870-
1924

childhood on this estate and, as the child of a landowner, benefited from a private education at home.

The background of Lenin's father, Ilya Nikolaevich Ulyanov, is on the face of it more straightforward. Ilya came from the city of Astrakan in the Volga delta, where his father Nikolai, the son of a serf, was a reasonably successful tailor and where Ilya was brought up as an Orthodox Christian. Nikolai's wife, Anna Alexeevna, was also presumably Russian but one of Lenin's sisters, echoing a family conviction, believed there was a non-Russian component to the Astrakan relatives and that Nikolai's wife had a Tatar (or Tartar) background. The Tatars, a Turkic-speaking, non-European, Muslim people, were once masters of a steppe empire which had included Russia until near the end of the 15th century. Ivan the Terrible had annexed their land in the 1550s but Tatar nobility were respected and accepted as equals. Since then, however, notions of innate Western superiority over non-Europeans had worked their way into the thought of the Russian ruling classes and Asiatics were looked down on as inferior and backward.

Tatars provide only one possible background for Lenin's paternal grandmother. She has also been identified as a Kalmyk, a Buddhist people, or possibly a Kirgiz, a Turkic-speaking, Mongolian race from Siberia and now called the Kazakhs. The Kalmyks and Kirgiz were nomad people of west Asia whose resistance to Tsardom had been broken by the mid-19th century and their land had been colonised and absorbed into the Russian Empire.

Lenin is usually portrayed as so quintessentially Russian that it is tempting to speculate over the exotic ingredients in his family history and ask whether aspects of his nature were genetically disposed by way of his ethnic plurality. While this is impossible to know,[4] one can certainly wonder if the cocktail of cultural backgrounds provided by these ethnicities helped create a childhood milieu more stimulating than one of a traditional, less hybrid family. Such a generalisation only opens up a somewhat abstract possibility and there is no evidence that the Ulyanov children were consciously made aware of heterogeneous elements in their family background. What is not in doubt is the kind of family values that the young Vladimir imbibed as a child in the Ulyanov household in Simbirsk.

The young boy who would become the revolutionary Lenin grew up in a family that placed a high value on the benefits of education, independence and self-discipline. His maternal grandfather, Alexander Blank, had become a doctor and retired as a serf-owning landowner under whom 40 peasant families toiled until their national emancipation in 1861. Emancipation by no means deprived him of all his land and he was able to enjoy a comfortable retirement on his estate, Kokushkino, outside of Kazan on the Volga. The sister-in-law with whom he came to live was an educated woman who had been taught to speak German, French and English by private tutors. They brought up Maria and her siblings in a fairly strict but supportive atmosphere, one that helps in understanding the kind of values that Maria helped create for her own children, including Vladimir.

Ilya, the man she married, had also been taught to appreciate the benefits of a self-improving and disciplined approach to life. His father having died when he was a child, his older brother, Vasili, had worked hard and sacrificed his own advancement to finance Ilya's progress through secondary school and university. When Ilya and Maria started their own family they too created a warm and secure environment for their children, one which inculcated a life-long respect for learning, hard work and purposive commitment to one's values.

The work of a conscientious school inspector for Simbirsk province – covering an area twice the size of Wales or Massachusetts – was arduous and demanding. A system of state schooling had been laid down by Tsar Alexander I (r. 1801–25) but its expansion had to wait until the reforming Alexander II (r. 1855–81) initiated a period of liberalisation. As well as the emancipation of serfs, forms of local self-government were introduced, autonomy was granted to criminal courts and there was a rapid expansion of primary schools. Ilya took his responsibilities seriously and travelled the length and breadth of the province, supervising the building of new schools, training teachers, monitoring standards, and journeys by horse-drawn carriage or sleigh entailed lengthy absences from home. His industriousness was rewarded when he was promoted in 1878 and the increase in income facilitated his family's move to a new and larger house in Moscow Street, in a prestigious neighbourhood in the centre of Simbirsk. Here, the young Lenin grew up in a large but very close-knit family. Anna was his older sister by six years and Alexander his older brother by four. He had a younger sister and brother, Olga and Dmitri, born when he was still an infant, and he was eight years old when the youngest in the family, Maria, was born in 1878. Their childhoods were happy ones and they grew up in reasonable comfort. A nanny, a cook and a gardener were on hand and each summer the family decamped for country pursuits with their relatives on the Kokushkino estate. The Ulyanov household was conformist and respectable, home to seemingly model citizens in terms of the Tsarist order, and the children retained a sense of family loyalty and solidarity that must have been nurtured by their parents. Ilya and

Maria were also at one in their keen desire to raise children who would be educated and resourceful, able to think and work methodically, apply habits of diligence and a studious imagination to the task at hand. Just what this would lead to for the two older brothers could not have been predicted by their parents or anyone else.

The two boys were close to one another and while Vladimir, nicknamed Volodya by the family, was the more noisy and energetic he naturally looked up to Alexander or Sasha, as the family called him. 'It got to be one of the jokes of the household that he would always reply, "*Like Sasha*," when a question was put to him such as whether he wanted his cereal with milk or butter.'[5] Edmund Wilson, who recorded this piece of family lore in *To the Finland Station*, visited the Ulyanov's house in the 1930s after Lenin's sisters had recreated its original interior. Mahogany furniture, a grand piano (Vladimir was taught by his mother how to play the piano), potted rubber plants and white curtains exude middle-class sobriety, maps and globes encourage the art of knowledge and, upstairs in the boys' adjoining bedrooms, school books on the shelves and nails on the walls for their towels.

'[Bedrooms in the Ulyanov house] look out on a little balcony, where morning-glory vines, trained on strings, screen it in with their purple-pink flowers. Beyond it is the apple orchard, which had been one of the most delightful features of the new house on the Úlitsa Moskóvskaya. The crowing of a neighbour's rooster is the only sound that breaks the silence of the provincial afternoon.'

Edmund Wilson, *To the Finland Station*[6]

This orderly and comfortable home, characterised by a warm but emotionally restrained atmosphere, helped create a stress-free environment which enabled the Ulyanov children to grow up with a sense of confidence and an inquisitiveness which made them receptive to new ideas. Although

Vladimir's closest relationships were always with members of his own family, there were others of the same age to play with. There was skating on the frozen Volga in winter and, at night, chess and family games. In summer there was fishing, swimming, country walks to gather mushrooms, and picnics with the samovar. The older Lenin could look back with political correctness to carefree days with his cousins in the countryside at Kokushkino. *I remember with pleasure how I used to loll about in haystacks, although I had not made them, how I used to eat strawberries and raspberries, although I had not planted them, and how I used to drink fresh milk, although I had not milked the cows.*[7] The parental stress on the importance of education meant that Vladimir, like his older sister and brother, was well-prepared for the start of his formal schooling at the age of nine. Their mother taught them to read and write and private tutors were hired to coach the children in preparation for the tests that determined entry into the town's two elite secondary schools, one for boys and one for girls. Vladimir, like Maria and Alexander before him, passed the tests and at the age of nine he donned his military-style school uniform and proudly took his place at the Simbirsk Classical Gimnazia. The curriculum was demandingly academic and the teaching of dead languages was heavily promoted by the government, with Latin accounting for nearly a third of the first-year timetable, classical Greek introduced in the third year and a half of pupils' final two years was spent translating Greek and Latin classics into Russian. French, German, Maths and Physics were also core subjects, the arts were largely ignored, and the key heuristic principle was rote-learning.[8]

Vladimir was intelligent and willing to learn and parental support, let alone expectations, ensured he did well. Alexander was achieving academic success at the school and this spurred on Vladimir to emulate his brother's scholarly achievements. Homework was unrelenting but what could have been punishing demands on a youngster's time were relished rather than resented. When his secondary education was over Vladimir's headmaster Fyodor Kerensky's final report on one of his most high-achieving pupils was full of praise for the son of Ilya and Maria Ulyanov: 'Quite talented, invariably diligent, prompt and reliable, Ulyanov was first in all his classes, and upon graduation was awarded a gold medal as the most meritorious pupil in achievement, growth and conduct. There is not a single instance on record, either in school or outside of it, of Ulyanov evoking by word or deed any adverse opinion from the authorities and teachers of the school.'[9] Fyodor Kerensky's own son, Alexander, was 11 years younger than Vladimir and in 1917 would head the Provisional Government that Lenin was determined to overthrow. Like the priest at his baptism, the headmaster might have been less effusive if he could have known whom he was endorsing.

The headmaster could control what was being taught in his school but not what was happening in the minds of his pupils. The stirring of the imagination and the arousal of curiosity in his prize student – activities strictly outside the school curriculum – came from the cosmopolitan and cultured milieu at home where authors like Gogol and Turgenev were read and discussed by the Ulyanov family. *We did not know hunger or cold; we were surrounded by all kinds of cultural opportunities and stimuli, books, music and distractions.*[10] Ilya and Maria were loyal and dutiful citizens but they were not philistines and their interest in writers deemed too liberal to be officially approved of was part of a home environment which filled some of the gaps left by the intellectually curtailed curriculum of the classroom. Vladimir's favourite novel was *Uncle Tom's Cabin* and it is a persuasive notion that his young, receptive mind might have been early provoked into critical reflection by a tale about slavery and the dying hero's resistance to oppressive power.

Before Vladimir left school, two deaths shattered the peace and calm of his secure and supportive family life. The first occurred over the Christmas holiday of 1885, when everyone was at home except Alexander. The oldest son was now a student at St Petersburg University and with exams coming up had decided to stay in the capital. Anna was also in the city, training to be a teacher, and she made the journey home to be with her family. Christmas passed peacefully, everyone attending church on 25 December, but early in the new year Ilya fell ill and within 48 hours he was dead from what seems to have been a brain haemorrhage. The funeral took place on 15 January and Vladimir helped carry the coffin; his older brother was not present, the family fearing the consequences of interrupting his crucial revision programme. After the funeral, there would be time for all the family to get together at Kokushkino and Alexander could bring his books with him and continue to study. It was a time for the family to rally round and deal with the shock of the unexpected – Ilya was only 53 when he died – and with characteristic efficiency Maria dealt with the practical matters. She applied for the pension, 100 roubles a month, that she was entitled to as the widow of a state official who had completed 25 years' service and arranged for part of her house to be rented out to a lodger. Alexander and Anna continued their studies in the capital, Vladimir was approaching the end of his secondary education and the three youngest children needed the care and devotion of their mother.

There was no financial crisis but emotionally it was a difficult time for everyone and especially so for an adolescent. Vladimir became withdrawn and taciturn, difficult in a way he had never been before, and he sought refuge in the reading of fiction. He had regularly attended Orthodox church services with his father and it was around this time that he lost his religious faith. Sixteen in April 1886, he was at a sensitive age and the premature death of his father must have been a heavy blow. Very soon after, and far sooner than anyone of his age could have been expected to, he suddenly found himself having to draw on all the mental strength and resourcefulness he possessed. The young Vladimir, having come to terms with the loss of his father, was now confronted with the horror of having his older brother executed by hanging for plotting to assassinate the Tsar. No one in the family had been aware of Alexander's anti-government politics and only after his death did Vladimir begin to put the political pieces together and come to understand what had led his brother to act the way he did.

The liberalising reforms of Alexander II which had so facilitated the career of Ilya Ulyanov had been of limited success for the country as a whole and the Romanov dynasty had not increased its popularity or secured a firmer basis for its continued existence. The emancipation of the serfs left the peasantry feeling justifiably short-changed – the gentry retained a lot of the best land and peasants had to make payments for what they received – and disturbances in the countryside were not uncommon. An agrarian socialist movement developed and some of its adherents, with a belief in violent direct action, succeeded in assassinating the Tsar in 1881. This put a halt to any further reforms and the reactionary new Tsar, Alexander III, ushered in a period of repression. The powers of the self-governing local assemblies introduced by his predecessor were reduced, the universities were subjected to more rigid control and any political concessions that might weaken autocratic rule became a remote possibility. Russia's intelligentsia, which included students, were hemmed in and dissent was monitored by the Ministry of the Interior which controlled the police and the Okhrana (security police). The Ministry, developing a widespread, international counterintelligence system using informers, agents provocateurs and officials who intercepted and read mail, implemented the anti-liberal policies of the Tsar. The activities of radical students were under surveillance and, although a group at St Petersburg University that included Alexander Ulyanov had not been infiltrated, the Ministry was alert to the threat of political assassination.

For Alexander, student life in the capital was as regimented and narrow as his school days in Simbirsk but he was older now and able to think and act for himself. He came to feel, as did many of the country's intelligentsia, that there was something fundamentally wrong with Russian society. The universities became hotbeds of radical dissent as a new and better kind of society was envisaged. Tsardom was seen as the major obstacle and, in the absence of any legitimate outlets for political and social criticism, opposition could take extreme forms. This was the case with the radical group that the 20-year-old Alexander joined in St Petersburg and towards the end of 1886 he committed himself to its plan to assassinate the Tsar. He was studying science at university and applied himself to the task of making the bomb that was planned to dispatch the Tsar as he made his way by carriage from the Winter Palace on the first day of March 1887 for a ceremony commemorating the sixth anniversary of the previous Tsar's assassination. The group hoped that the killing would focus people's discontent and with this in mind proclamations, to be issued after the assassination, were prepared in advance.

On 1 March, some of the conspirators were observed on Nevsky Prospect, the capital's main thoroughfare, where they had been seen the day before, and they aroused the suspicions of the police.[11] They were arrested – the bomb was in their possession – and interrogation by the Okhrana led to the arrest of nearly all the members of the group; Alexander's involvement caused his sister Anna to be also brought in for questioning. She was released when her innocence was established but Alexander, realising he could not hide his complicity, chose to make a political stand during his trial in April. He stood up to the judge and explained that terrorist opposition had been brought on by a wilfully intolerant government. A death sentence was unavoidable, although his mother did everything possible to save him, petitioning the Tsar and travelling to the capital to beg her son to show remorse and hope for a lesser sentence. The idealistic Alexander refused to bend and at dawn on 8 May he was led with four of his fellow plotters from his cell to a prison scaffold and executed.

While their mother was pleading for Alexander's life in St Petersburg, the Ulyanov children were at home struggling with raw and painful emotions. Their middle-class neighbours and acquaintances viewed them as pariahs[12] – posters proclaiming Alexander's perfidy were publicly displayed around the town – and for the first time in his life Vladimir experienced rejection. The Ulyanov spirit, however, was strong and responded to the challenge facing them. Vladimir, just 17, did his best to control his feelings and played games with Maria and Dmitri to help them cope. As with his sister Olga, vital school examinations began in early May and if Vladimir was to qualify for a university place he would have to sit them and do well. Not aware of the fact, he took an exam on the day Alexander was executed and carried on sitting them for a week after the death was announced. It took remarkable powers of concentration and self-control on the part of Olga and Vladimir to deal with their predicament and emerge from the month-long examination schedule with the highest marks in their years. Their father would have been proud of them.

There are two accounts of what Vladimir said in response to his brother's act of terrorism. The version that came from his sister Maria, the one officially endorsed and often repeated – *No, we must not go down that road* – is most probably apocryphal. It came to be favoured by Soviet authorities because it fitted in with the notion of a politically precocious Lenin distancing himself from the inadequate politics of Alexander and his conspirators. This seems unlikely because Vladimir was not yet reading political material, and Maria was only eight when she is said to have heard him make this remark. A more convincing account is the one recorded by one of the few acquaintances who did not ostracise the Ulyanovs, a family friend and teacher who helped the children with their school work. Her memory of what Vladimir said – *It must mean that he had to act like this; he couldn't act in any other way*[13] – suggests a troubled teenager trying to comprehend and come to terms with what his brother did. It also suggests an understanding of, and natural sympathy with, the nature of Alexander's personality. He was a highly principled young man who convinced himself that killing the Tsar would bring about social and political progress for the people of Russia and that therefore regicide was ethically correct. Alexander helped write his group's statement that included the words:

'Convinced that terror results wholly from the absence of a minimum of freedom, we can state with complete confidence that terrorist activities will cease, if the Government grants this "minimum of freedom".'[14] The sincerity of Alexander's attitude, and this is what his younger brother could respond to, is apparent from his refusal to seek clemency and the explanation for this that he gave to his mother: 'Imagine, Mama, two men facing each other at a duel. One of them has already shot at his opponent, the other has yet to do so, when the one who has shot asks him not to. No, I cannot behave like that!'[15]

Maria Alexandrovna, deeply shocked by the death of her son, returned to Simbirsk in a feeble state of mind, close to being traumatised. The realisation that the remainder of her family badly needed her support helped her pull back from the brink. In her absence, her sister Anna had returned home to help look after the family – the youngest child, Maria, was not yet ten – and it was a time for everyone to pull together. For Maria Alexandrovna, her life had undergone a tragic reversal of fortune. Happily married and in her middle age, materially and socially secure, with caring children whose bright prospects must have warmed her heart, a period of little over two years had shattered this peace of mind for good. Now widowed and with her eldest son executed in the prime of his life, the rest of her life would be characterised by a seemingly endless series of journeys and changes of home in efforts to support her remaining children.

Vladimir's future was one of her immediate responsibilities and Maria Alexandrovna must have felt relieved and grateful for the final school report that Fyodor Kerensky wrote for his star pupil because it was instrumental in securing her son's admission to Kazan University. As the brother of a terrorist, a place at the prestigious St Petersburg university attended by Alexander was out of the question but one of the seven other universities in the Russian Empire was at Kazan, on the Volga and less than 125 miles away from Simbirsk. Kerensky's report, stressing Vladimir's good behaviour and the loyal, pious nature of his parents, helped convince the authorities that if his mother agreed to live in Kazan, so that the young Vladimir would be at home while attending university, he would not follow in the ways of his brother. So, in the autumn of 1887, the family moved to Kazan, the schoolboy became an undergraduate, and Vladimir began a new chapter in his life. It would be a very short chapter.

Lenin and Krupskaya first met in 1894. This photograph shows them together in Gorki in 1922.

What Was to be Done?

The Tsarist state, taking for granted its right to rule without a parliament or political parties, regarded its absolutism as an unquestionable principle of government. In joining an illegal conspiracy, Alexander had been following those who had earlier sought political change in Russia. This revolutionary lineage dated back to December 1825 when a group of Russian officers, imbued with the radical sentiments flowing through Western Europe as a result of the French Revolution, attempted a *coup d'état*. Tsardom's reaction to those rebels, the Decembrists, also set a pattern for the state's future response to opposition. The army was ordered to open fire on demonstrators, individuals were singled out as leaders and executed while others were sentenced to lengthy jail sentences or exiled to Siberia. Repression was severe at times and even the discussing of revolutionary ideas, as Dostoyevsky and other members of a literary group found out in 1849, could lead to a death sentence.[16] Following Russia's defeat in the Crimean War (1854–6), some reforms had been initiated by the Tsar but they failed to deal with agrarian discontent, and the country's intelligentsia looked to radical solutions.

The perceived need for social and political change that

arose in the 1860s, later becoming known as Populism, was never a coordinated grouping and was sometimes more of a cultural mood than a political movement. Different, variously named clandestine groups were formed and what they shared was an affinity for loosely defined notions of agrarian socialism. Looking to the collective nature of the Russian commune and seeing it as a model for a more egalitarian form of society, Populists sought to remove the exploitation that held back the socialist potential seen as inherent in the types of rural organisation practised by the commune system. The first Populist group of any significance, Land and Freedom, emerged in the mid-1870s and a schism soon emerged within it between those looking to acts of violence as a catalyst for immediate change and those who preferred a gradualist, propagandist approach. One of the leaders of the non-terrorist group was Georgi Valentinovich Plekhanov, someone who would later become an important influence on Lenin. Some of those who disagreed with the approach of people like Plekhanov formed the People's Will and carried out the assassination of Tsar Alexander II in 1881, unwittingly inaugurating a period of severe repression against all forms of opposition. The group that Alexander Ulyanov belonged to was itself an offshoot of the People's Will, resurrecting its strategy of removing the Tsar in the belief that this would act as a prelude to a general revolt.

The Populist attitude to capitalist development, which recognised it as an emerging force within Russia but which did not see it as an essential stage in the progress towards socialism, also produced disagreements within the intelligentsia. Populism tended to idealise the peasantry, viewing capitalism as an alien and destructive force to be kept at bay, and this strain of socialist thought had little in common with mainstream European Marxism. An increasing number of Russian radicals, driven out or self-exiled in Western Europe, took up the ideas of Marx and saw how they could be applied to Russia in the context of the rapid industrialisation that was taking place in their home country. Some rejected any reliance on terrorist acts and saw their task in terms of spearheading an organised working class movement. Others, most notably Mikhail Bakunin, sought not to turn their back on the terrorist tradition and remained committed to the value of spontaneous acts of violence while simultaneously bringing libertarian perspectives to bear on Marxist thought. The man who would emerge as Lenin was the inheritor of both these radical strands.

Vladimir was awakened to a new level of consciousness as a direct result of his brother's execution but he did not suddenly become a Marxist activist, nor did he immediately adopt Alexander's political outlook. He had very little idea of how his brother had been thinking in St Petersburg and Alexander's daring activism had come as a shock to the schoolboy in Simbirsk. Driven by the pain of loss and the remembrance of the older brother he had so admired, Vladimir was curious and needed to know what had led Alexander to risk and then sacrifice his life. He took out some of the books that were still in Alexander's St Petersburg lodgings

Mikhail Bakunin (1814–76), born near Moscow, participated in the German revolutionary movement in 1848 and promoted a libertarian brand of socialism while remaining addicted to authoritarian forms of organisation in the personal pursuit of revolution. His historic break with Marx in the First International set the terms for a bitter dispute between anarchists and Marxists and, although their strategic differences were deep-seated ones, they shared a belief in the need to replace capitalism with socialism. Bakunin's influence was greatest in France and Italy; and in Spain the impact of his ideas played an important role in the development of anarchism in that country.

and began to turn their pages. As he read, he began to feel and share some aspects of his brother's outlook and this process of identification was as much an emotional as an intellectual progression. The book that made most impact on him was not a political tract but a work of fiction that he had first tried reading when he was 14. Nikolai Chernyshevsky's *What Is To Be Done?* now stirred his imagination in a way it had not done before – and it is not difficult to see why. The novel's fidelity to the emancipation of the spirit is astonishing and its belief in human goodness and the possibilities for improving the human condition is inspiring. The novel's plot gets underway with the character of Vera Pavlovna, a girl from a poor family who escapes the clutches of her exploitative mother when she meets Lopukhov. Their socialist ideals unite the pair of them in a seemingly sexless but politically passionate marriage. When Vera falls for her husband's friend, her spouse selflessly and spectacularly endorses the relationship. The commitment to a communal lifestyle, championed throughout the novel, represents a triumphant rejection of old values in favour of a new attitude towards life. Subtitled 'Tales of New People', the novel imaginatively celebrates modernity and the heroes in the book are quite unlike the Hamlet-like characters, grappling with perplexities of the national soul, that are more familiar from Russian literature, as this excerpt shows. 'Come up out of your godforsaken underworld, my friends, come up. It's not so difficult. Come out into the light of day, where life is good; the path is easy and inviting. Try it: development, development. Observe, reflect, read those books that tell you about the pure enjoyment of life, and about the fact that man can be kind and happy. Read them: such books gladden the heart. Observe life: it's so interesting. Reflect: it's so fascinating. That's all there is to it! No sacrifices are needed, no deprivations required – they're all unnecessary. Desire to be happy – that's all. Only desire is needed. To attain it you'll take delight in devoting yourself to your own development. That's where true happiness lies. Oh, what delights accrue to the developed individual! Even things that another person experiences as sacrifice or sorrow, he experiences as satisfaction and enjoyment. His heart is wide open to joy and he has a great deal of it. Try it – it's good.'[17]

The impact of reading *What Is To Be Done?* was profound and the novel's title would later be borrowed by Lenin and used for his own, first declaration of revolutionary fervour. He remarked to a friend how reading the Populist writer *ploughed him over and over*[18] – the image suggesting a creative upheaval in his mind – and Chernyshevsky seems to have been the single most important influence before he began reading actual Marxist works. Though a novel that is stylistically unimpressive and easy to criticise, the idealistic commitment of the young characters in *What Is To Be Done?* engaged Vladimir's emotions – evoking the dignity of his brother's refusal to beg for the Tsar's mercy – and he went on to read the non-fictional writings of Chernyshevsky. He wrote to the author, a photograph of whom he treasured, and was disappointed when there was

Nikolai Gavrilovich Chernyshevsky (1828–89), the son of a priest, attended St Petersburg University and, his plans for an academic career stymied by his post-graduate supervisor, took up the offer of a permanent post as a journalist in a radical magazine. He published a number of literary and philosophical essays that brought him to the attention of the authorities and in 1862 he was arrested and confined in the Fortress of St Peter and Paul in the capital. It was here that his novel *What Is To Be Done?* was written, before he was convicted of subversion, largely on the basis of trumped-up evidence. He served seven years hard labour followed by permanent exile in eastern Siberia. After 18 years, broken in health and spirit, he was finally released but he died soon after.

no reply, not knowing Chernyshevsky was dying. The young Lenin was deeply affected by engaging for the first time with a materialist, socialist philosophy that clearly distinguished itself from liberalism.

The fact that Marx set about learning Russian in order to read Chernyshevsky suggests how highly he was regarded in European radical circles. What would become more significant, however, was the influence Marx himself was having in Russia. The first foreign-language edition of *Capital*, in Russian, had been published in 1872 and it was not banned because the censor judged it too indigestible to have any undesirable effect on readers. In the course of the 1880s, Marxism was embraced by a section of the intelligentsia that had witnessed the failure of Populism. Russian intellectuals responded to an analysis of society that looked not to the peasantry for change but to the class of workers engendered by industrialisation. Belatedly when compared to Western Europe, this class was now visibly emerging in Russian cities and capitalism generally was seen as a 'progressive', evolutionary development that would take the country out of its retarded feudalism and advance it towards socialism in the way that Marx outlined.[19]

Marxism and Populism pointed in two very different directions for activists in Russian revolutionary circles, and it was Marxism that emerged as the dominant influence. The kind of socialist parties that were developing in Western Europe, especially in Germany, came to represent the way ahead for Russian radicals. By the time Vladimir was reading Chernyshevsky, the German Social Democratic Party, taking its doctrines from Marx, was the largest socialist party in the world and in 1890 won 35 seats in the Reichstag. Such a mass party was out of the question under Tsardom and, because any activist openly agitating for one faced arrest and imprison-ment, Russian Marxists usually found themselves forced into exile. One such former Populist, Plekhanov, left for Switzer-land in 1880 and three years later helped form with his fellow intellectual Pavel Axelrod an embryonic Russian Social Dem-ocratic party. When the Second International held its inaugu-ral meeting in Paris in 1889, Plekhanov was there to speak as Russia's representative Marxist.

The International Working Men's Association – the First International – was founded by Marx in 1864 and, though for-mally dissolved 12 years later, came to an effective end in 1872 when a split between Bakunin and Marx divided its Congress at The Hague. At the launch of the Second International in 1889, by which time anarchists were on the margins of the offi-cial socialist movement, working to gain power in national par-liaments was endorsed as a legitimate strategy. May 1st was proposed as a common date for mass demonstrations in favour of the eight-hour day and there was unanimous agreement that working-class parties would oppose any war between capitalist governments.

Georgi Valentinov Plekhanov (1856–1918) emerged from Populism to develop the first Marxist perspective on Russia's political and social development. Hounded by the secret police and aware that his chances of avoiding imprisonment were slim, he left Russia in 1880. Three years later, he played a vital role in founding the earliest Russian Marxist organisation, the Emancipation of Labour group, and later became the leader of the Russian Social Democratic movement. Worshipped by the young Lenin, ideological differences led later to a split between them. Plekhanov finally returned to Russia in 1917, a marginal player in the revolution.

In the autumn of 1887, Vladimir knew very little, if any-thing, about the First International or Russian Marxist circles in exile in Western Europe. He knew that he did not want to follow his brother by studying science or, as his teachers expected, the classics. He was going to Kazan University to study law and become a lawyer. It was not a propitious time, however, for a new student to immerse himself in academic study at Kazan. There was unrest in the university, students and teachers were under surveillance, and when a protest was organised in December – it seems to have been little more than a gathering of disaffected students – Vladimir was identified as one of those present. In the wake of a crackdown by the authorities, with troops brought into the city, the odds were stacked against leniency being shown towards the brother of an infamous revolutionary. Vladimir was informed he would not be allowed to finish his first term.

His mother, once again, did everything she could to secure the best terms for one of her sons at the mercy of the authorities. Permission was given for Vladimir to stay at the Kokushkino estate, if his mother remained with him, and he spent the winter there wisely keeping his head down. It could only be a temporary arrangement because Vladimir, whose expulsion from university gave time for a prolonged burst of reading subversive material, was experiencing a growing sense of alienation. His mother was desperate to find some way of continuing his education and she also had the problem of what to do with Dmitri and Anna, who had been enrolled in Kazan schools. Maria Alexandrovna wrote letter after letter and finally secured permission for the family to resume residence in Kazan, though a return to university was ruled out for her errant son.

Vladimir was developing politically and his expulsion from university only hardened his hostility to Tsarism. He joined underground meetings of dissidents in Kazan. Perhaps his mother sensed the need to get him away from the city. She purchased a small estate at Alakaevka in Samara province, situated to the south and further down the Volga, and in May 1889 the Ulyanov family once more moved home in the hope of a better future. Emotionally it was a trying time for Maria Alexandrovna but at least there was financial security. The new estate had been purchased using funds accrued from the sale of her Simbirsk house and money left by her husband. Her father, Alexander Blank, had died and having inherited a share of his Kokushkino estate she was also receiving some money from that source. In Samara, she hoped that Vladimir would take to life in the countryside and become a working manager of the estate; prospects were even better for the rest of her children. Anna wanted to become a teacher and Olga a doctor, while Dmitri and Maria would settle into secondary schools in Samara.

The development of the political consciousness that would turn Vladimir into Lenin began around 1888 and continued with a new intensity during his time in Samara. He devoured everything written by Chernyshevsky that he could get hold of and, moving on to the writings of Plekhanov, was introduced to the ideas of Marx. It is around this time, 1888–9, that Vladimir first read Marx. He warmed immediately to his interpretation of history and the significance he attached to the transforming power of capitalism. Vladimir was won over by Plekhanov's insistence that Marx showed how radical change in Russia would not come from the peasantry but from new economic forces in the form of a bourgeoisie and, its nemesis, an emerging urban working class. Such an analysis did not ignore or minimise the importance of unplanned revolutionary moments, like the sudden eruption of discontent that created the Paris Commune of 1871, but it did mean that opposition needed to be prepared and organised in advance for such events. Conditions in Russia were different to those prevailing in countries like Germany, where a Marxist-inspired Social Democratic Party could operate legally, and Vladimir could concur with Plekhanov's unwillingness to categorically renounce terrorism as a means of bringing down Tsarism. What Alexander Ulyanov had attempted to do was not wrong, politically or ethically, but as a strategy it was of limited use and his younger brother could see himself working towards a more effective way of completing the unfinished business. Vladimir's politics were developing, a process not an event, and Lenin was slowly but surely emerging.

His mother's hope that her son would look after the new estate came to nothing. Details are hard to come by but it seems that his managerial efforts were short-lived, failing to fulfil the desires of a young man whose interest was more in books than bullocks. He was relieved when within a few months of moving into the house at Alakaevkas the family shifted to a house in the town of Samara. Vladimir was quick to join a clandestine group of young intellectuals in the town and his political education continued. He read more Marx and Plekhanov and, convinced by their class-based dissection of capitalism, he began to weave together an analytical politics of the real with the fervent idealism of Chernyshevsky's fictional characters. Vladimir was still a young man, not yet 20, and ideas were swirling about in his mind. He would sometimes take off on his own for days at a time and sail a boat down the Volga before returning to Samara. *How I miss the Volga*, he wrote years later when feeling low in Paris.[20] In Samara, he may have felt frustrated, living at home and barred from university, and he shared his mother's conviction that without some formal qualifications his prospects in life were dismal. Together, they pleaded with the authorities and in May 1890 permission was given for him to enrol as an external law student. In August of that year, having chosen St Petersburg as the university to register with, he left home for a three-month period of study in the capital and prepared for examinations that would take place a year later.

Vladimir had no intention of messing up his second chance of gaining a degree and he worked as assiduously as he had back in secondary school in Simbirsk. When he was studying in St Petersburg he had the company of his sister Olga who was also a student in the capital and planning to travel abroad to fulfil her ambition to become a doctor. It was not to be. She contracted typhoid and died on 8 May 1891, aged 19, on the anniversary of her brother's execution four years earlier. It was another terrible blow to the Ulyanov family but they bore it with the same fortitude that had helped them manage previous losses. Vladimir had always been close to Olga, they had sung 'The Internationale' together in French and enjoyed time together in St Petersburg walking by the Neva and watching ice-breaking machines at work. Now he had to arrange her funeral and after her burial he returned with his mother to Samara. After Alexander's execution, Vladimir and Olga had forced themselves to concentrate on school exams that were pending; now, without his sister, he spent the summer preparing for the law exams scheduled for that autumn. He passed with flying colours, gaining the equivalent of a first-class degree in law, having never attended lectures or tutorials and in less than half the time normally taken; testimony to a fine intellect and tremendous powers of organisation and dedication.

He could now make a living as a lawyer and, having found a post as a trainee in Samara, began work early in 1892. He also resumed his contacts with Marxists and continued to read and study, political and economic material proving far more absorbing than law books. Many modern accounts of his life at this time are keen to stress how he could depend on his mother's income to support his growing radicalism. This is true to some extent because his family did not live a hand-to-mouth existence and Maria Alexandrovna did want to do everything possible to help her children. At the same time, it seems unfair to blame the yet-to-emerge Lenin for not living according to beliefs that would in time account for his remarkably frugal and principled approach to life.

Within 18 months of qualifying as a lawyer, at the age of 23, Vladimir Ulyanov was ready to turn his back on what could have been a successful and prosperous career as a lawyer. The family made a decision to leave Samara and in the summer of 1893, with Dmitri having completed his secondary education, plans for a journey by steamer on the Volga had once again been finalised; not further south but northwards towards the capital. Maria Alexandrovna, now in her late fifties, with Anna, Dmitri and Maria, would find a place to rent in Moscow; her oldest surviving son, still known to his family by his childhood nickname Volodya, was heading back to St Petersburg on his own, where he would mostly be known by his surname Ulyanov.

The population of St Petersburg, a city built on swampy ground where the Neva river disgorged the waters of Lake Ladoga, exceeded the million mark when Ulyanov returned there in August 1893. Peter the Great, the Tsar who in the early 18th century had ordered every stonemason in the Russian Empire to work on building his grand new capital, had succeeded in creating a city that looked out towards Europe. When the rebel Decembrists demonstrated in the city around the statue of Peter the Great in 1825 their political orientation was also westward looking. By the end of that century, St

Petersburg was the natural setting for Chernyshevsky's 'New People' to express themselves; it was also the city where their author had created them, in solitary confinement inside the Fortress of St Peter and Paul.

The largest metropolis in the Empire, St Petersburg was awakening as a powerhouse of Western industrialisation. Factories like the Putilov Iron Works counted their employees by the thousand and throughout the 1890s unemployed peasants poured into the city and were transformed overnight into badly-paid, disaffected workers. The city was becoming a crucible of urban discontent, fuelled by a raw capitalism that was, paradoxically, subsidised by an aristocratic Tsarist government. The paradox arose because Tsarism knew it had to encourage industrial development, hence the tempting subsidies it offered to foreign capital, but hoped it could do so while retaining political control and a social order firmly fixed in the past.

St Petersburg was also the cultural and intellectual capital of Russia and it was this dimension that made it the natural destination for Ulyanov. Its libraries, bookshops, discussion groups and small publishers fed his appetite for ideas and arguments about Russia's future course and he became increasingly absorbed with books and with writing. On 5 October, he wrote to his mother to let her know he had at last found suitable lodgings, only 15 minutes from a library and quiet enough for him to study. In the letter he tells her he has visited Olga's grave and reassures his mother that the cross and wreath are intact. He requests some money because his funds are low and explains how he is waiting for 70 roubles owing to him from a legal case he had undertaken in Samara. He asks about the state of his mother's finances and enquires whether she has received the rent due from the Alakaevka estate. He then provides a detailed breakdown of his expenses for his first month in St Petersburg (38 roubles after essential, one-off expenses) and berates himself for having spent too much: *Obviously I have not been living carefully; in one month I have spent a rouble and 36 kopeks on the horse trams, for instance. When I get used to the place I shall probably spend less.*[21] Ulyanov comes across in the letter as a self-contained young man, careful about money and solicitous for his mother. Effusiveness is never a characteristic of his personal letters but concern for his family is clearly evident. In the same month, he replies to a letter from his younger sister Maria – *I have not been to the Hermitage Museum or to theatres. I somehow do not want to go alone. In Moscow I shall be glad to go to the Tretyakov Gallery and other places with you.*[22] – wanting to know about her progress at school and asking how Dmitri is getting on with his studies. He writes to her again in December to ask once more about her schoolwork, advising her to balance homework with exercise and recommending a daily two-hour walk, and follows this up with another letter advising her to follow her doctor's advice and miss school until she is feeling better.

Ulyanov liked to talk and he began to be noticed for his argumentativeness and command of detail in discussions with fellow Marxists. In February 1894 he attended a meeting where a young woman, Nadezhda Krupskaya, remembered his sardonic laugh at what he saw as a lame suggestion for working with a literary committee. It is not known if Ulyanov noticed the woman with whom he would share the rest of his life but it seems unlikely and it was the end of the year before they were in a meeting for the second time. Krupskaya's father was a disaffected army officer who served in occupied Poland and later passed into the civil service. His career came to an end when his daughter was five years old. He faced internal charges – the details are lost but his patriotism was questioned – and was banned from public service. After 1874, Krupskaya was moved around with her parents, often living with her mother in her various posts as governess. The family moved to St Petersburg in 1880 and Nadezhda, whose name means Hope, entered a prestigious girls' school. She graduated with distinction from the school in 1887, four years after her father's death, and developed an interest in reading which opened her to influence by the radical intelligentsia. She took a teaching job in a school for adult workers and met Marxists on the staff.

She and Ulyanov got to know one another over the winter of 1894–5, took walks together and talked politics in Krupskaya's apartment where she lived with her mother. Anyone noticing them walking together along the banks of the Neva would have seen an attractive young woman[23] with a boyfriend who looked much older than his years but not unhandsome in his own way. He had already lost much of his hair, the effect being to emphasise his forehead and suggest erudition and seriousness, but his trim, reddish beard was a youthful one.

Ulyanov, away from home for good, found himself and his life's direction in the years 1894 and 1895. The intellectual energy and intelligence that in other circumstances could have made him a distinguished academic were applied to understanding how capitalism was developing, primarily in Russia, and how it could be replaced by a system that would lead to communism. There was no going back to Populist dreams of agrarian socialism, such fond notions had to be hit on the head, but the commitment of those radicals in the past who sought to remove Tsarism was an ongoing inspiration, as was their realisation that a ruling class does not voluntarily relinquish its power. A revolution was necessary but the practical realisation of this was not at hand and, in the meantime, the task was to study, write and correct misleading ways of combating the existing order. A movement based around the working class was essential and Ulyanov could contribute to its creation while also working as a lawyer, though soon his professional training would be laid aside in the interests of working towards a revolution.

Ulyanov had undertaken his first piece of writing in Samara in 1893, analysing economic statistics on agriculture, but the liberal magazine he submitted it to was not interested. At the end of 1894, for the first time, he used a pseudonym when putting a name to a Marxist review he wrote that was accepted for publication in a book, though in the event the Ministry of the Interior prevented the book's circulation. Up until now, the Ministry had also been blocking his request for a passport but in the spring of 1895 this changed and Ulyanov seized the chance to travel outside of Russia. As an official representative of Marxist groups in Russia, he was delighted at the prospect of making contact with Plekhanov in Switzerland and on a personal level he was excitedly looking forward to meeting one of his intellectual heroes. He also wanted to play the tourist and see some of the world outside of Russia. His meeting with Plekhanov in Geneva went well and he also spent a fortnight with Pavel Axelrod, Plekhanov's associate, in Zurich. Travelling on to Paris, where he rented a room, he hunted down Marx's son-in-law Paul Lafargue, and he also looked up other Marxists in Berlin and Vilnius. It was the end of September before he returned to St Petersburg, his dedication to Marxism reinforced and his optimism buoyed up by firsthand contact with like-minded intellectuals across Europe.

Ulyanov's first experience of travel outside of Russia was also important in terms of his personal development. He experienced the shock of realising that the German he had learnt in school as a foreign language sounded like one to the native speakers with whom he attempted to communicate. He loved the Swiss Alps, deepening his enjoyment of country walks and the open air, and when he found a spa where the doctor had a good reputation he cast aside budgetary restraint and splashed out on a course of treatment for an ongoing stomach ailment. He kept in regular contact with his mother by mail and more than once asked her to send him 100 roubles. The month before leaving for the return journey, he had enough money left over to ask if there was anything he could buy for the family that would be cheaper in Berlin's large shops. For Dmitri, he proposed a medical book that might help him in his studies but he could not think of what to buy for Maria and asked his mother and Anna to suggest something suitable.

Ulyanov returned to St Petersburg in September 1895, not only with presents for his family but with illegal literature secreted in a specially-made double-bottomed trunk. He was acquiring other tricks of the dissident's trade and these included methods of writing in code and using invisible ink, means of communication that would be put to practical use in the wake of his unexpected arrest early in December. The Ministry of the Interior's interest in the activities of Ulyanov was aroused when his Marxism, up till now confined to discussion groups, moved up a gear and engaged itself with the concerns of industrial workers. This came about due to the arrival in St Petersburg of Yuli Martov, a Jewish Marxist who was three years younger than Ulyanov but politically more advanced in that he argued for involvement in industrial disputes as a way of engaging with workers on their own terms. With this in mind, a new group was formed and Ulyanov, who got on well with Martov both personally and ideologically, began applying his writing and research skills to the task in hand. Workers were on strike in a St Petersburg textile factory and Ulyanov wrote a propaganda leaflet and a pamphlet outlining legislation governing aspects of the workers' conditions of employment. For the first time in his life, mainly through Krupskaya's contacts with workers, Ulyanov engaged personally with the working class. Preparations also got underway for the publication of a newspaper targeting workers. This was exactly the kind of activity the Okhrana wanted to nip in the bud and they set about finding an informer and targeting members of the group. This did not take long and on the night of 8 December Ulyanov was arrested and detained for questioning.

Ulyanov was not unduly shaken by his arrest and adopted a philosophical but practical attitude towards his situation. His group had proved itself vulnerable to the Okhrana and in future tighter security would be necessary; in the meantime, he would make the best of his imprisonment. He established what his rights were as regards receiving books and being allowed to write and then set about planning a piece of research that had been on his mind. He would require a large number of books for his subject matter, the nature of agriculture in contemporary Russia, and reliable people on the outside would have to organise the delivery and return of library books. By January 1896 he had a preliminary reading list compiled. Once again, his mother rose to the occasion and moved to the capital with her daughter Anna so that they could be at hand and render assistance. There were two visiting days each week and his mother and Maria came on one of them for the allotted half-hour, Anna on the other, longer, visit but speaking through a grille. They delivered so much food to his cell that he could joke about it in a letter to his sister.[24]

Ulyanov was kept in detention for over a year, over which time Martov, Krupskaya and others were also arrested, and his surviving prison letters of 1896 reveal something of his character. He has a superb sense of organisation and command of detail – right down to requesting the kind of pencil that will not depend on his wardens' goodwill in getting it sharpened – and does not, in writing at least, feel the need to express passing moods or engage in introspection. He is courteous and kind, thanking friends for their help and apologising to Anna for the demands he is making on her. He is 26 years old and his arrest, far from dampening his political outlook, is taken in his stride as an occupational hazard. As someone who has involved himself with striking workers and contributed to literature supporting their cause, he is not surprised to be arrested and held for a year while his fate is decided by the government. He will learn from the experience, organise with more circumspection in the future and work against Tsarism in a better-prepared state. Much of the time was spent in solitary confinement and there were spells of aching loneliness. He sent a coded message to Krupskaya, before she was arrested, asking her to be at a certain spot outside the prison at a designated time so as to catch a glimpse of her during his exercise period. Heart and mind worked together to make the best of the situation.

By February 1897 the authorities, acting as judge and jury, were ready to hand down sentences on the agitators they had arrested and Ulyanov received three years' exile in Siberia. This was not as harsh as it may seem and would have been worse if his offence was considered more seditious. Ulyanov was subject to a period of banishment from mainstream life, not confined to a prison or a camp, and providing he did not cause any trouble and followed the terms laid down then he would be left alone to pursue his own interests. If prisoners had the necessary funds they could apply for permission to organise their own transport to Siberia. Ulyanov was success-ful in this and able to plan a leisurely journey into exile.

Although Ulyanov was not given to expressing his feelings in writing, it does not mean that he went into exile without misgivings. He was being punished for political beliefs that outside of Tsarist Russia would not result in an enforced sep-aration thousands of miles away from his family and quite possibly in a harsh and physically challenging environment. He said goodbye to Dmitri in Moscow, having being allowed to break his journey there for a week, before travelling on by train in the company of his mother and two sisters as far as Tula, some 125 miles south of Moscow. At Tula station, he parted company with them and boarded another train for the journey eastwards. At this stage, he still did not know his final destination and remained in the Siberian city of Krasnoyarsk for two months. He was not bored in Krasnoyarsk, for other exiles had been domiciled there and he could talk politics, although reading newspapers in the library that arrived 11 days after their date of publication was something he could not get used to. A new train service would reduce the journey time from St Petersburg to eight days, he noted with approval in a letter to his sister. He also visited a local magnate who was famous for his private library, and was invited to make use of his books; the one-hour walk there on foot was just the kind of exercise Ulyanov enjoyed. He tried to make the city of Krasnoyarsk his place of exile on medical grounds, citing a doctor's confirmation of his stomach complaint, and although this request was turned down his special pleading was rewarded when he was finally allocated to Shushenskoe, a large village to the south and with a population of 1,500. He heard the news early in April and was delighted. To reach Shu-shu-shu, as he first called it, took at best four days by steamship on the river Yaeniesi and then a day's travel by road – the return journey for post to and from the capital would take at least a month – but it was not the most uncongenial corner of Siberia, despite winter temperatures of 20° and more below zero, and some fellow exiles would be in the vicinity. He would receive a monthly allowance of eight roubles – the poorer workers in St Petersburg were earning half this – to buy food and rent accommodation and, supplementing this, he expected payment for articles he had written. It was not the Swiss Alps but the snow-capped Sayan mountains were visible in the distance, there was woodland, opportunities for shooting game and a nearby river to bathe in. His cheerful letters to his mother and sisters in 1897 suggest his deep relief at not being condemned to some awful outpost near the Arctic Circle, as happened to his friend Martov, and soon Ulyanov is busy once again using Anna to order research materials for the book he had begun writing in the remand prison. He is pleased to hear that his mother and Anna are taking a summer holiday in Europe and that the Kokushkino estate is finally being sold.

By the autumn of 1897, his initial ebullience was wearing thin – *today you take a walk to the right of the village, tomorrow to the left; today you write one article, tomorrow another*[25] – and with winter approaching there was the prospect of a lonely existence. In the first month of 1898, he requested permission for Krupskaya, who had been sentenced to exile in Ufa province in the Ural Mountains, to serve her time in Shushenskoe on the grounds that she was his fiancée. Krupskaya made her own submission to the Ministry of the Interior and also asked for permission for her mother to accompany her. This last request was unusual and adds to the uncertainty about the nature of the relationship between Krupskaya and Ulyanov at this time. Krupskaya's mother was a devout Orthodox Christian and she may have been concerned about her daughter living 4,000 miles away with Ulyanov. If so, her worries were put to rest when it became clear that the authorities would insist on a marriage taking place without delay. Ulyanov's future wife and mother-in-law arrived in Shushenskoe in early May but it was July before all the paperwork was ready and then the marriage took place in the local church. The priest insisted on a wedding ring and this was supplied by one of the two other political exiles in Shushenskoe, a man who was hoping to set himself up as a jeweller. To assist him in this endeavour, Ulyanov had asked Krupskaya to pack a jeweller's kit in her luggage and this was put to use in the fashioning of two copper rings.

Their Siberian honeymoon lasted nearly 18 months and in retrospect it seems like an enforced idyll in Ulyanov's life. Krupskaya's observation – 'We were newlyweds, you know – and brought beauty to this exile. If I did not write about this in my memoirs, that does not mean that there was neither poetry nor youthful passion in our life' – has a ring of truth to it and her reticence to dwell on their emotional togetherness is more than matched by Ulyanov's brief, almost business-like references to Krupskaya in the regular letters he wrote to his family during this period. What is known, though, suggests a happy time for both of them. They went swimming and walking together and Ulyanov could show off his skating skills in winter. He rather fancied himself as a sharpshooter when it came to bagging game[26] and the longest letter he writes to his brother Dmitri is taken up with details about the kind of gun he would like him to buy on his behalf. Ulyanov got on well with his mother-in-law and a young domestic help was hired – her pay was two and a half roubles a month – who lived with them in the cottage and Krupskaya taught her to read and write. When writing to his relatives, Ulyanov comes across as he did in his letters from the remand prison: courteous, concerned for others, prudent about money and punctilious in organising his scholarship. He was writing a book, numerous articles and doing some translation work, and with no library to visit his research needs presented a challenge. Ulyanov was a professional scholar, telling a sister that without proper proof-reading there was no point in publishing anything. He was once tempted by the extravagance of subscribing to a new edition of Turgenev's works, hoping that a payment due for a translation could justify the splurge. Always careful about money, he was aware of debts to be paid and depended on irregular payments from publishers in order to make ends meet.

Ulyanov was concerned about Dmitri's fate when, in late 1897, his younger brother was himself arrested and became a political prisoner, though getting off lightly by being banished only to Tula, to the south of Moscow. He wrote to his mother: *It's bad that in two and a half months he [Dmitri] has already begun to look puffy. First – does he stick to a diet in prison? I suppose not. In my opinion that is essential. Second – does he do physical jerks? Probably not, either. Also essential. I can at least say from my own experience that with great pleasure and profit I did my gymnastics before going to bed. You loosen up so well at times that it makes you warm even in the worst cold, when the cell is like an ice-well, and after it you sleep better, I can recommend to him an exercise that is very convenient (even if funny) – bow to the ground 50 times. I set myself that stint and was not embarrassed when the warder watched me through the peephole and was amazed that a prisoner who had never expressed a desire to attend the prison church should suddenly have become so pious! He must bow not less than fifty times without bending his legs and must touch the floor with his fingers each time. Tell him that.*[27] Even by comparison with this, though, Ulyanov's time in Siberia was not especially onerous. There were no personal, professional or financial burdens to bear, no difficult decisions to make, he was happily married and with his wife, and their neighbours and acquaintances were friendly and undemanding, police surveillance was minimal (the house was searched only once) and there was time to study, write and to think. Ulyanov was keeping up to date with developments within Marxism and, noting revisionist trends that threatened to dilute the need for revolutionary change, was keen to return to the fray. When his period of exile came to an end so too did a period of his life when he had been more of a scholar than a revolutionary. Now though, Ulyanov knew that he was returning to the real world and he sensed what needed to be done. It was time to become Lenin.

A police photograph of Lenin in 1905.

Becoming Lenin

Marx identified class interests and the conflicts they gave rise to as providing the underlying dynamic of history and for Ulyanov there was no compelling reason to turn away from this fundamental insight into the nature of society. A numerically small class of rulers could wield enormous political and social power and under capitalism such a class would rule in the interests of capital and private wealth and at the expense of the broad mass of people whose labour largely produced this wealth. Different governments would cloak this class rule in different ways, and with varying degrees of enlightenment, but an underlying conflict between class interests would remain, as would the need to work towards the creation of a different kind of society. In Ulyanov's first book, *The Development of Capitalism in Russia*, which was completed in Shushenskoe and published in 1899, he could not say anything like this explicitly and get it past the censors but he could work indirectly towards it and get the message across. Marshalling an impressive range of economic data, Ulyanov's book drove home the argument that capitalism was changing the nature of Russian agriculture and turning the poorer peasants into landless workers who had to sell their labour in the countryside, just as the proletariat had to in the cities. Russia was developing an economy indistinguishable from those of Western Europe and what was left unsaid, but clearly there between the lines, was the conclusion that Russia was experiencing the same class conflict that characterised those societies. The downfall of obsolete Tsarism was predictable but so too was the likelihood that it would be replaced by a government representing capitalist interests.

A key line of argument that challenges Marxism, as much today as when it first appeared in Ulyanov's time, asserts that there is no irreconcilable division between the classes and that this is evidenced by the progressive amelioration of the poorer sections of society. The lives of working people can be gradually improved by legislation, raw capitalism can be moderated and the wealth it creates distributed in socially responsible ways. Revolution is not necessary and an evolution towards socialism, or at least a more equitable and less divisive society, is possible by trade unions campaigning for economic reforms. When such thinking reached Russia, it was castigated by Marxists like Plekhanov and labelled Economism by its detractors. Lenin was quick to recognise the threat that such revisionism posed to Marxism and, as his exile in Siberia drew to a close, he became increasingly anxious to play an active part in combating such ideas by reaching out to workers.

Russia's working-class was numerically small – 2.7 million workers were permanently resident in towns and cities in 1905, though the total number was swelled by peasants who migrated seasonally into factory employment – but highly concentrated. In 1901, the year after the end of Ulyanov's exile, some 30 per cent worked in factories with more than 1,000 employees and this percentage was increasing. With wages kept low and housing conditions horrendously inadequate, the degree of workers' disaffection was also growing, Workers were crammed like battery hens into tiny rooms, often sharing beds on a shift system, or forced to eat and sleep on the floor next to the machines that they worked for up to 11 ½ hours a day, the legal maximum, and often a lot longer.

Ulyanov wanted to start a newspaper representing the Emancipation of Labour group that Plekhanov had formed in Switzerland, and reach Marxist activists in the cities of Russia. The challenge was to establish, finance, distribute and maintain such a newspaper in the face of the repressive apparatus of the Tsarist state. In January 1900, Ulyanov's banishment to Shushenskoe came to an end but his freedom remained so drastically curtailed – forbidden to live in any large city, confined to the provinces and under police surveillance – that he was still effectively in exile. His initial destination was Podolsk, south of Moscow, where his mother was now living, while Krupskaya had to travel to Ufa, over 600 miles east of Moscow, to serve out the remainder of her term of exile. Ulyanov chose to reside in Pskov, south of the capital, but while in St Petersburg on an illicit visit he was arrested and spent over a week in prison. Life was clearly going to be difficult for him in Russia and, when the Ministry of the Interior granted permission for him to leave the country, he made immediate plans to travel to Switzerland. Once there, he could discuss with Marxists his idea for a newspaper. Before his departure, he travelled to Ufa to spend some time with Krupskaya and to say goodbye until her detention came to an end and she could meet up with him in Europe. From a letter Ulyanov wrote to his mother in April, it is clear that Krupskaya had been diagnosed with a gynaecological problem and confined to bed for a period of weeks. It cannot be known for sure but perhaps this helps explain why their long-lasting marriage produced no children. Ulyanov was concerned for his wife's health and applied, unsuccessfully, for permission to spend six weeks with her during her illness in Ufa.

Matters did not proceed smoothly in Switzerland either. Ulyanov is characteristically reticent about personal matters and this makes all the more surprising his willingness to express in writing how hurt he was by what happened when he met with Plekhanov. The elder Marxist was revered by Ulyanov but Plekhanov, sensing the young man's challenge to his leadership role among Russian expatriate Marxists, proved extremely prickly when it came to organising the editorial board for the newspaper. In the remarkably frank 'How the "Spark" Was Nearly Extinguished', written in September 1900, Ulyanov gives a detailed account of the traumatic breakdown in their relationship, registering the shock of discovering his idol's feet of clay. Plekhanov's display of peevish pride and his suggestion that Ulyanov and a colleague were mercenary careerists jeopardised the whole newspaper project. A disillusioned Ulyanov listened to Vera Zasulich, one of the co-editors, pleading with him not to break with Plekhanov – *It was, indeed, so painful that at times I thought I would burst into tears*[28] – and, though matters were patched up, a serious break had occurred. It was agreed to print the newspaper in Munich, so Ulyanov set off for Germany to get the project off the ground and the first issue of *Iskra* ('The Spark') was printed at the end of 1900.

By the spring of the following year Krupskaya was able to join her husband in Munich and soon after her mother also arrived to live with them. Ulyanov was busy working on a booklet that he would publish in 1902 under the name of N Lenin – a pseudonym already used by him in some letters

– and the work would become the first of his major pieces of writing. The inspiration for its title, *What Is To Be Done?*, came from Chernyshevsky and in answering his hero's question he laid out a set of concerns that would lead to the creation of the Bolshevik Party. By spelling out how to effect the right kind of political change, the author also outlined a programme for political action that has helped create the pejorative use of the term Leninist.

What Is To Be Done? is a combative response to Economism and its dilution of Marx's key insight into the uncompromising class nature of society. It repeats an assertion first made in *Iskra*'s editorial statement that *before we can unite, and in order that we may unite, we must first of all firmly and definitely draw the lines of demarcation.*[29] Theory is important, Lenin insists, because in its absence there will be no sure guide as to how to act in the future. Economism plays down theory in the interests of pragmatism but a flexibility that is too elastic will become an excuse for backsliding. *There are politics and politics*[30] and the kind of politics that deals only with the exigencies of the moment will slip into a reactionary opportunism and lose sight of the ultimate aim to challenge Capital and create a different kind of world. The consciousness of large numbers of working people will not be raised by just focusing on narrowly defined economic issues like rates of pay and conditions of work, important though these be, and Lenin calls for a broader awareness of society: ... *of the landlord, of the priest, of the high state official and of the peasant, of the student and of the tramp.*[31] The necessary awareness will be nurtured by intellectuals and activists who are not themselves workers in a factory and all classes of people will be involved in the struggle to change society. Education and enlightenment will not naturally emerge from the workplace, hence the crucial need for an organisation, a party, that can take on the task.

It is the final section of *What Is To Be Done?*, dealing with the organisational form of the party, that has become the best known and most reviled part of the text. What is needed, argued Lenin, is a vanguard of cadres that can lead working people to a realisation of the need for revolutionary change. Membership of this vanguard party cannot be open and in no way can it be a broad organisation of workers – hence the charges of elitism and authoritarianism that have become synonymous with the term Leninist. What is sometimes forgotten, though, is the Russian context of a repressive, autocratic state where any kind of opposition was illegal and where a political police force worked successfully to identify and imprison dissidents. Weak organisation within the group his elder brother had belonged to had not helped its cause and the three-year exile of the author of *What Is To Be Done?* was itself the result of police infiltration and poor organisation. Indeed, the average life of a Marxist group in turn-of-the-century Russia, before the police intervened, was estimated at three months.[32] What was the point of struggling to overturn Tsarism when revolutionaries could so easily be arrested and brave young men like his brother Alexander lose their lives? The large mass of people will determine the final outcome of the struggle ahead, agreed Lenin, but combating the political police demanded a highly organised, professional approach on the part of a small group of dedicated revolutionaries. Such a group was elitist in so far as it was made up of professional revolutionaries, Lenin readily agreed, but this was a matter of organisational necessity. Similarly, such an organisation had to be undemocratic because it could not hold public elections and had to remain clandestine. These conclusions had been reached during his exile in Siberia. Organisation was paramount and, in order to raise consciousness, a newspaper was essential, as was the right kind of relationship between the public and the clandestine party group.

What Is To Be Done? was enthusiastically received by many activists in Russia who were waiting for just such a rallying call to decisive action. Trade unionism alone would not change society, nor was it a matter of waiting for historical forces to take their natural course; Lenin, breathing fire, preached success if only the right approach was adopted and rigidly adhered to. *Give us an organisation of real revolutionaries and we shall overturn the whole of Russia.*[33] Lenin was appealing to the heart as much as the head – *We should dream*[34] – heroically calling for extraordinary dedication and discipline, promising the reward of the overthrow of autocracy.

While the Russian context helps account for Lenin's ideas on party organisation, his premise that a properly focused mass consciousness – capable of sustaining a transformation of society – will not arise spontaneously is a general one he regards as applicable to all class-divided countries. The forces of conservatism are too well resourced and developed, too clever at isolating acts of opposition and using trade unionism to corral and curtail discontent, for a radical consciousness to naturally emerge as a matter of course. In *What Is To Be Done?*, Lenin anticipates and welcomes the legalisation of trade unions in Russia but stresses how this will only accentuate the need for a party of revolutionaries who will advance the struggle politically and take it beyond the gradualism inherent in trade unionism. In 'Letter to a Comrade on Our Organisational Tasks', written in 1902, Lenin set out in theoretical detail how this party would work and structure itself. Operating clandestinely in the Russian police state, it would necessarily possess a highly centralised leadership but, equally necessary as a corrective to the power of this nucleus, it would be informed by a highly decentralised structure that kept communication open with the mass of party members. Lenin thought he could have his cake and eat it. Centralised leadership came down to a small group of totally committed individuals possessed of the necessary energy, talent and experience, but the concentration of power this created was not problematic because power would be kept in check by a decentralising structure that networked together the mass of party members. The party, he wrote, would be like a well-conducted orchestra, everyone playing the instrument they were best at, harmoniously following the conductor. It would swell to a size previously unimagined, the music would grow thunderously loud and demand to be heard, but to reach the revolutionary pitch the conductor's guidance and a military-style sense of discipline were essential prerequisites.

The vital role of *Iskra* was to help provide the musical score for the revolution yet to come and Lenin's immediate task was to keep the newspaper in existence. There was a danger that the Munich printing press would be closed down by the police and this forced a move from Germany. Along with the other younger members of the editorial board, Yuli Martov, Alexander Potresov and Vera Zasulich, Lenin was reluctant to base the paper in Switzerland where the older two editors, Plekhanov and Axelrod, lived. London suggested itself as a viable alternative and in April 1902 Lenin and Krupskaya arrived there, their contact being an *Iskra* comrade living at 14 Frederick St, near Gray's Inn Rd. This comrade, Nikolai Alexeev, had arranged for them the rental of a two-bedroomed, unfurnished flat at 30 Holford Square, not far from his own address. The other three editors took rooms, also not far away, in Sidmouth Street. A sympathetic printer had also been found, at 37A Clerkenwell Green, a half-hour walk away from Holford Square. With the British Museum equally close by, everything was conveniently located and a good start to living in London had been made. Life got better for Lenin and Krupskaya. They gradually mastered the language, enjoyed walks in Hyde Park and picnics in Primrose Hill and grew accustomed to English ways while relishing the cosmopolitanism of a world city. Early in 1903, they attended a Sunday concert in Queen's Hall, 320 Regent Street, to enjoy a performance of Tchaikovsky's Sixth Symphony with Henry Wood conducting, and Lenin wrote to his mother saying how much he had enjoyed it. The Ulyanovs continued to keep in close contact with one another and in the summer of 1902 a family holiday was organised in Brittany, with Anna and her mother travelling to France to spend some time with Lenin.

In London, Lenin walked most mornings to the Reading Room of the British Museum[35] while Krupskaya, aided by her mother who came to live with them again, handled secretarial work for *Iskra*. There were always letters that needed coding or decoding – from St Petersburg, Moscow, Samara, Kiev, Nizhni Novogorod, Baku, Vilna, Riga and many other cities – and this work was handled by Krupskaya.[36] The actual printing of *Iskra* in London was a straightforward task but the process of transporting an illicit newspaper to Russia and then distributing it within the country so that it could be reprinted involved elaborate and risky procedures. There were secret postal routes to organise and passwords and various codes for the comrades handling the transport and distribution. On the whole, the operation was remarkably successful given that 51 issues were published during Lenin's time on the editorial board in 1900–3 and that each issue involved the operation of a complex distribution system. The Tsarist secret police could not interfere with the legitimate printing of a newspaper in another country but they were keen to prevent subversive material reaching Russia and, for this reason, engaged in counter-intelligence work to the extent of having a foreign headquarters in Paris. This accounts for the cloak-and-dagger aspects of Lenin's life abroad: the use of pseudonyms, safe houses for postal deliveries, false passports and forged identity papers, invisible ink and various codes. Krupskaya remembered one comrade, with a reputation for forging documents, who came to London and had all the tables in the Sidmouth Street flat turned over to act as presses for forged passports. Trotsky recalled the smell of burnt paper, from the secret letters heated over a fire to reveal their contents, in the Holford Square flat.

Editorial work on *Iskra*, printed every fortnight, took up a lot of Lenin's time and he was also regularly contributing articles for the newspaper. The ones he wrote on political strategy gave *Iskra* an intellectual weight while events of importance in Russia, like the trials of workers brought to court for participating in protests, were also reported and commented on by Lenin. The speech of Pyotr Zalomov, made at his trial in October 1902, became well known across Russia and was quoted in the newspaper: 'I joined the demonstrators consciously, but do not admit any guilt, since I believed I had a right to participate in the demonstration, which was protesting against all those laws that, while protecting the interests of the privileged class of rich people, do not provide for the workers any opportunity to improve their living conditions ... . That is why I wrote on my banner: "Down with autocracy and long live political freedom!"'[37]

Lenin worked hard to make *Iskra* the undisputed voice of Russian Marxism. On most days he spent at least a couple of hours at the rooms in Sidmouth Street where the other editors lived and worked, until the autumn of 1902 when their landlord asked them to leave. They were renting five rooms on two floors and, by all accounts, it was rarely kept tidy; but what most made it anathema to Lenin was the lack of privacy. *I should go mad if I had to live in a commune*, he reportedly said in reference to Sidmouth Street and, agreeing with a sentiment expressed by Chernyshevsky, insisted that *everyone has a corner in his life which should never be penetrated by anyone, and everyone should have a special room completely to himself.*[38] During this time, Lenin also made a number of short trips to continental Europe, addressing meetings and networking within Russian émigré circles.

Leon Trotsky (1879–1940), born Lev Davidovitch Bronstein, became involved in revolutionary activities as a teenager and, like Lenin, was exiled to Siberia for his efforts. He escaped in 1902, fled to London and joined the Russian Social Democrats. He did not join the Bolsheviks until May 1917 but went on to play a major part in the October revolution. Founder and commander of the Red Army, his influence waned after the death of Lenin and in 1927 he was exiled by Stalin to Central Asia. In 1929 he was expelled from the Soviet Union and finally found asylum in Mexico where he was assassinated by one of Stalin's agents.

In between work and leisure time, there were unexpected Russian visitors to the Holford Square flat, like the young man who had escaped from Siberia and knocked on their door early one morning in the autumn of 1902. His pseudonym was Leon Trotsky and he arrived with a reputation as a 'real young eagle' whose fluency as a writer had earned him the nickname 'the Pen'.[39] He made such a good impression that within a few months Lenin proposed that he join *Iskra*'s editorial board. Plekhanov was not impressed – 'I don't like the pen of your "Pen"'[40] – and blocked the nomination.

Lenin was happy to remain in London but Martov, seeking to mend the divisions in *Iskra*'s editorial board, proposed moving the newspaper's operation to Switzerland. Lenin's objections were overruled by the other editors and he had no choice but to comply. In order to keep on top of the situation, this meant packing up books and belongings in April 1903 and leaving a contented life in London for new accommodation in Geneva.

The Second Congress of the Russian Social-Democratic Labour Party was being organised for the summer of 1903, to take place in Brussels, and Lenin threw himself into the work of preparing for this. The party had been formed in Minsk in 1898 by nine activists who called their inaugurating meeting the party's First Congress. Their Marxists roots had been laid down by Plekhanov's Emancipation of Labour group, formed five years earlier in Switzerland but, following swift arrests by the police, their organisation existed more in name than substance. Meanwhile, the Populist tradition re-emerged with the founding of the Socialist Revolutionary Party in 1901 and, with liberals in Russia also beginning to organise themselves, it was time to assert a more organised Marxist position. This was the purpose of the Second Congress: to put the party on its feet, establish a constitution and begin making its presence felt within Russia.

Differences of opinion with Plekhanov, emerging this time over the programme for the Brussels conference, once again caused real distress for Lenin and manifested itself in bouts of insomnia. His health suffered and he succumbed to an infection that kept him in bed for two weeks in Geneva. The political spats that awaited Lenin in Brussels would be relegated to academic footnotes were it not for differences of opinion that came to have enormous significance for the future. Martov wanted a more inclusive definition of party membership than the one proposed by Lenin and the debate that followed caused a breach within the *Iskra* group. Lenin wanted a party that restricted membership to ideally full-time members but Martov and his supporters won the vote on the wording of a definition for party members.

However, following the departure of some delegates,[41] Lenin and his supporters were now able to form a majority amongst the voting delegates and, as with the earlier dispute over the definition of a party member, what became important was a matter of semantics. Formed from the Russian word for majority, 'Bolshevik', became the term adopted by Lenin for those supporting his position – at this stage it would be premature to speak of a faction – while the Russian word for minority, 'Menshevik', was unwisely accepted by Martov as the term for his bloc of followers. It was unwise because it suggested Martov's position was a marginal one, outside the mainstream, at a time when allegiances were fluid and far from fixed. At the time, though, Martov was unsuccessful in opposing Lenin's proposal that *Iskra*'s editorial board be reduced to three, even though Martov would be one of the triumvirate. Along with a small central committee, the *Iskra* board would be under the control of a centralising party council. There were many arguments, and battle-lines were being drawn up. Lenin's nerves became frayed, his insomnia returned and he lost his appetite – annoying his landlady by not eating the Dutch cheeses and radishes that she prepared for breakfast. To add to the difficulties of the Congress, all the delegates had to decamp from Brussels at short notice when a worrying degree of police surveillance necessitated a change of venue. The decision was made to shift the Congress to London and it was in Charlotte Street that the first sitting took place. Such was the secrecy surrounding the meetings, the various venues for the subsequent sittings remain unknown.

Bickering and brokering continued for months after the formal end of the Congress and the rift between Bolsheviks and Mensheviks only deepened, despite various attempts to patch up differences. Plekhanov began to take the side of Martov, as did Trotsky, and matters reached a head when Plekhanov sought to co-opt back onto the *Iskra* board the three members who had earlier lost their positions. Lenin, unprepared to compromise, handed in his resignation from the *Iskra* board and the party council. It was an intrepid, characteristically bold decision, perhaps a tactical mistake he would come to regret, but he was determined to stick to his guns. He began writing a pamphlet, *One Step Forward, Two Steps Back*, giving his account of the schism in the party, and re-entered the fray by getting a sympathiser to co-opt him onto the party's central committee.

Consisting of only 43 delegates with voting rights, the Second Congress and its split was hardly headline news across Europe. For those at the heart of the squabbling, however, there were principles to defend and positions to advance. Lenin, experiencing stress that he had largely brought on himself, sought reassurance by recalling with Krupskaya a simile that they remembered reading in Tolstoy. The figure of a man is seen in the distance, squatting on his haunches and gesticulating frantically with his hands. He appears to be demented but, when viewed closer, is actually someone sharpening his knife on a paving-stone. Lenin knew he was reacting extremely to disputes within the party but, convinced that it was vitally important to get the politics correct from the beginning, was prepared to accept being regarded as a mad outcast.

These were trying times for Lenin, a man who put his heart

and soul into his politics. News from Russia informed him that both of his sisters and his brother Dmitri had been arrested and detained by the Okhrana, and he wrote to his distressed mother to keep her spirits up. By the summer of 1904, it was his own spirit that needed cheering and he knew he was badly in need of some rest. When he set off with Krupskaya for a month's walking holiday in the Swiss mountains, where he took to sleeping ten hours a day and stopped reading, he was possibly on the edge of a nervous breakdown. It was probably the first time since early childhood that he allowed days to pass without reading a book or newspaper of some kind. He lightened his mind, and his rucksack, by sending back to Geneva some of the books he was carrying, retaining his Switzerland *Baedeker*, and the workaholic gave himself up to the fresh mountain air and day-long treks. He gradually recovered, buoyed up by hearing his sisters and brother had been released from prison. Obviously enjoying the carefree, outdoor life and his time with Krupskaya, he sent a holiday postcard to his mother with *Greetings from the tramps*.[42]

When they returned to Geneva early in September 1904, a reanimated Lenin was ready to take on the Mensheviks. He had a new ally in the young intellectual Alexander Bogdanov, who proved invaluable in raising funds, and together they launched a new newspaper to rival the now Menshevik-controlled *Iskra*. In Russia, as the author of *What Is To Be Done?*, Lenin had his share of dedicated supporters and with their help he was able to rebuild a network of agents and consolidate the Bolshevik position. It is around this time that his uncompromising tenacity and strength of will asserts itself vigorously, winning many to his side, while to others he was displaying a dogmatism and intolerance that came to be seen as essential characteristics of the man.

While the political émigrés played their political chess games, events were unfolding back in Russia that would soon give them all a jolt. *Iskra* competed with other clandestine newspapers agitating for change and the Russian Social-Democratic Labour Party was not the only political group organising for the overthrow of Tsarism. The Socialist Revolutionary Party (SR), carrying out a number of assassinations of high-profile officials, made clear its own impatience at the continuing existence of autocracy. Liberal opposition to the rule of the Tsar, coalescing into what would become the Constitutional Democratic (Kadet) Party, was also hardening. Demonstrations and strikes were becoming more common than they ever were in the past, as was the sight of troops called on to quell the threat of disorder on the streets, and peasants were also beginning to express their discontent in the countryside. The more enlightened amongst the authorities acknowledged the need to respond to the changing situation by trying to channel the restlessness that was fuelling the activities of revolutionaries. The head of Moscow's political police initiated a policy, adopted by other cities, of recognising trade unions that confined their concerns to the economic sphere and which could, so the thinking went, be monitored and infiltrated more effectively by being out in the open and led by non-revolutionary leaders. The imperial court itself was looking at the position of the peasantry and once again considering reforms that would pacify their growing disgruntlement.

At this critical period in Russia's development, Tsarism could either adapt and emerge stronger or – and this is what did unfold – compound its errors and create a revolutionary situation that threatened its very survival. The first defeat inflicted on the reign of Nicholas II came not from militant insurgents but from the Japanese, and the Russo-Japanese War became a focus of discontent for an already discontented populace. The Japanese were regarded by many as militarily and racially inferior – Nicholas' predecessor dismissed them as 'monkeys who play Europeans'[44] – but they proved stronger and better organised than their enemy and inflicted a series of humiliating defeats on Russian forces. On the industrial front, at the huge Putilov Works plant in St Petersburg, a strike broke out at the end of 1904 and the organisation behind it was one of the police-controlled trade unions. Led by an Orthodox priest, Father Gapon, a large demonstration was arranged for Sunday 9 January 1905. Workers and their families would form a peaceful procession and walk to the Winter Palace in St Petersburg

The war between Russia and Japan brought victory, for the first time in the modern era, to an Asian force at the expense of a European army. The Russian Empire had always been expanding – between 1683 and 1914 at a rate calculated on average at 55 square miles per day[43] – but its occupation of Manchuria in 1900 brought it into a conflict with Japan that it came to regret. War broke out early in 1904 and by April Japanese troops had gained the upper hand at the land battle of the Yalu river. A Russian fleet was besieged in Port Arthur, precipitating the port's capture by the Japanese before the end of the year, while the Baltic Sea fleet set out on a 18,000-mile journey to Asia only to be defeated, with the loss of 5,000 men, in the Tsushima Strait in May 1905.

and hand in a petition calling for moderately expressed democratic rights. An orderly procession of over 150,000 people walked to the Winter Palace but were met there by troops who opened fire on the crowd, killing at least 200. The idealism of Father Gapon, initially working for the police, was transformed by Bloody Sunday and he declared the day after: 'We no longer have a Tsar. A river of blood divides the Tsar from the people.'[45] This marked a watershed in Russia's history. Protests mushroomed, strikes and demonstrations broke out in other Russian cities and it became clear that armed government force would not easily quell the discontent.

Lenin, like all the émigrés, was caught off-guard by the news of Bloody Sunday and the turmoil across Russia that followed. His limited knowledge of events, based at first on reading newspaper reports in Geneva, made it impossible to influence what was happening. He was, however, quicker than most Bolsheviks in sensing the importance of what was happening and he was elated to meet with the fleeing Father Gapon in Geneva and gain an insight into events on the ground. In April he left for London with Krupskaya, in preparation for the Third Congress of the Russian Social-Democratic Labour Party, and they took rooms at 16 Percy Circus. The Congress was organised by the Bolshevik-led central committee of the party and its purpose, as well as responding to the developments in Russia was, ostensibly at least, to try and unify the party. In the event, the *Iskra* Mensheviks, led by Plekhanov and Martov, refused to attend and Lenin himself chaired most of the sessions. Brushing aside criticisms of revolutionary adventurism and Jacobinism, Lenin and Bogdanov called for the organising of a political uprising. Lenin was in no doubt about the need for an armed insurrection and he urged forward violent opposition to Tsarism. The gulf between the Bolsheviks and Mensheviks was deepening.

Meanwhile, nation-wide demonstrations were developing across Russia, sailors on the battleship *Potemkin* mutinied and in the non-Russian borderlands large-scale strikes overlapped with nationalist protests. In the autumn of 1905, strike committees in St Petersburg evolved into an administrative body, a Soviet (Council), representing 250,000 workers and forming its own militia. Soviets sprung up in other cities and the mood was becoming more revolutionary – Trotsky rose to prominence in the St Petersburg soviet – and, starting in October, trouble spread to the countryside. Rent strikes and widespread disturbances, aimed at forcing landlords to abandon their estates, subsided with the onset of winter only to break out with greater ferocity in the spring of 1906. Reacting to such events, Lenin's thinking about political strategy was declutching itself from some Marxist pieties and striking out in new directions. The received wisdom was that a bourgeois revolution must precede a proletarian one but in Russia the bourgeois class might not be developed enough, politically and numerically, to take on this historic role with confidence and certainty. Lenin never denied the need for or the importance of a bourgeois revolution but he feared that in Russia it might too readily be absorbed by Tsarism and fatally weaken the prospects for proletarian intervention. Therefore, he argued, there should be a new kind of alliance, one that could establish a *revolutionary-democratic dictatorship of the proletariat and the peasantry*.[46] This development of the Marxist formula of the dictatorship of the proletariat, a notion which Marx had left very vague, would take shape as events continued to unfold and affect Lenin's thinking.

In October 1905, responding to what had become a national strike, the Tsar was reluctantly persuaded to issue a Manifesto, promising radical reforms and a Duma (parliament). It was time for Lenin to leave the safety of Geneva and enter the revolutionary fray, as Trotsky and Bogdanov had done, and accompanied by Krupskaya he left Switzerland for Sweden in November. In Stockholm, a ferry was boarded for Helsinki and from here, travelling separately from Krupskaya, he took a train to St Petersburg and reached the city's Finland Station on 8 November. The man who had left Russia in 1900 was Vladimir Ulyanov; it was Lenin who was now returning.

Revolutionary troops gather outside the Duma in St Petersburg during the
February 1917 revolution.

Bolshevik Blues

Lenin was wary about his open presence in St Petersburg, although he did register with the police for a short while, and early in December 1905 he and Krupskaya adopted false papers and often lived apart for security reasons. It was a busy period for Lenin. For the first time he met the novelist Maxim Gorky (1868–1936), a supporter of the party, and helped him, as an editor and contributor, with his *New Life* publication. Gorky was to go into exile following the government's recovery and repression of dissent. Working with Bogdanov, he established a school for Russian workers at his home on the island of Capri. Gorky did not always agree with Lenin and after 1917 the writer came into conflict with the Bolsheviks.

Lenin travelled to Finland before the end of the year to attend a Bolshevik conference and met there someone else for the first time, a delegate from the Caucasus called Stalin. In April of 1906 Lenin travelled to Stockholm for the Fourth Party Congress, a conciliatory affair which brought Bolsheviks and Mensheviks together despite the Bolsheviks keeping themselves organisationally separate. In May he addressed his first public meeting in Russia. As ever, he was constantly writing articles and pamphlets but time was still found to take a short holiday in July, outside of St Petersburg, with Krupskaya, her mother and his own mother.

In the autumn of 1906, Lenin moved to Kuokkala, only some 37 miles from the capital but across the border in Finland, a relatively secure location where police surveillance was not a constant worry. Finland was a Russian possession but self-governing in many respects, with its own border control and ferry routes to continental Europe, and a two-storey dacha at Kuokkala made a good base for leading Bolsheviks who now made up what became known as the Bolshevik Centre. Lenin, Krupskaya and her mother lived on the ground floor, Bogdanov and his wife moved in upstairs, and in January 1907 Maria Ulyanov visited for a while.

Kuokkala was on the St Petersburg–Helsinki rail line and it was convenient for Krupskaya to travel to the capital while Lenin, receiving news from Russia on a daily basis, wrote and organised from the dacha. Kuokkala remained his home for most of 1907 – it would take ten years and another revolution before Lenin would openly return to St Petersburg – for the volatile situation in Russia made security a real concern, and increasingly so as the government reasserted its control. An uprising had begun in Moscow only a month after Lenin had arrived back in Russia but the rebel areas were shelled by troops and throughout 1906 there had been fighting between soldiers and strikers; in the countryside, peasant disturbances were ruthlessly crushed. By early 1907, the result of massive repression and Stolypin's 'necktie' the uprising was seen to have failed. In the six months before April 1906, an estimated 15,000 people were executed and 45,000 deported or exiled.[47]

As far as the anti-Semitic Tsar Nicholas was concerned,

the defeat of rebel workers and peasants and, as he saw it, a conspiracy by Jewish radicals, proved how unnecessary it was to make concessions and he continued to believe that an undiluted autocracy could rule with impunity. His Prime Minister, Peter Stolypin, who sought to combine state terror with political concessions, had a more realistic grip on the situation. Stolypin's approach might have saved the monarchy, had he lived, though he struggled against the reactionary mind-set that Nicholas personified. After Stolypin, Tsarism continued but, lacking the support of the small but important bourgeois class and attracting the growing antagonism of a larger populace, its ability to survive was weakened by self-delusion and political short-sightedness.

The First Duma had sat from April 1906 until it was disbanded a few months later, after showing too much support for radical change. At first, Lenin called for a boycott of the parliament but when the Second Duma opened in 1907 he called for his party to stand separately and vigorously opposed Plekhanov's support for an alliance with the liberal Kadets. He also opposed a group of Bolsheviks, including Bogdanov, who called for the party to withdraw from the Duma and go underground. It was time to prepare

Appointed Prime Minister in mid-1906, Peter Stolypin (1862–1911) set about saving Tsarism by promoting agrarian reforms that would enable peasants to acquire ownership of the land. At the same time, as part of his attempt to nurture a conservative peasantry and inoculate it against the radicals, he sought to liberalise the process of electing local government councils. To deal with the threat of revolutionaries, however, he introduced a new court system that made it easy to convict dissidents and the result was some 3,000 executions: the hangman's noose became known as 'Stolypin's necktie'. Attending the Kiev Opera House in 1911, and neglecting to wear the bullet-proof vest that he often wore, Stolypin was shot twice by an assassin and died a few days later. His land reforms never became law.

for a defence of his position at the forthcoming Fifth Party Congress, planned to take place in Norway in April 1907.

The Norwegian government refused permission for the Congress, as did the Danish and Swedish authorities, and it was in London once again that the delegates met. The Congress was held from 30 April to 19 May, in the Brotherhood Church in Southgate Road, Hackney, courtesy of the socialist churchwarden.[48] In attendance were 336 delegates, Bolsheviks making up a clear majority, and the meetings proved sufficiently exhausting for Lenin to feel he needed a rest when they were over. After a short holiday with Krupskaya near Styrs Udde in Finland, it was back to business and Lenin was busy attending conferences, including a congress of the Second International in Stuttgart. The 1905 upheaval in Russia had once again raised issues of direct action, and in particular the role of mass strikes, for the European left. Syndicalism in France, Spain and Italy favoured the general strike as a way of undermining the status quo, while the German Social Democratic Party was becoming increasingly cautious about any kind of radical action. The use of anti-militarist strikes in the event of a war was argued over, as it had been at previous congresses, but this time Lenin and Rosa Luxemburg further radicalised the issue. They called for working-class action to seize the opportunity offered in the event of a war breaking out not only to oppose the hostilities but also to work to organise the overthrow of the governments. Such revolutionary motions were becoming anathema to many of the leading delegates, especially the Germans, but they went along with a wordy and imprecise resolution to this effect and it was unanimously adopted by the Congress. For Lenin and Luxemburg, a basis for socialist action against a war had been accepted.

Born in Russian Poland, Rosa Luxemburg (1871–1919) had become a German citizen in 1895 and took an active part in the German Social-Democratic movement. She emerged as one of the leaders of the left wing of the Second International and knew Lenin for a number of years. In the revolutionary turmoil in Germany in 1919, with Social Democratic leaders manoeuvring with the military to gain control, Luxemburg was seized by army officers and murdered.

Lenin returned to Finland after the Congress but the political situation in Russia was returning to its pre-1905 state and it was no longer a safe place for revolutionaries. The Second Duma was disbanded by Stolypin in June 1907 and his subsequent gerrymandering ensured that the Third Duma was under right-wing control. These constitutional changes signalled the defeat of the revolution and, with the hopes of activities dashed, Lenin and many others, retreated to the safety of Western Europe. There was now a new Bolshevik newspaper, *Proletari*, and it was decided to move its operation to Geneva and then Paris. If Krupskaya's account of Lenin's narrow escape from Finland is accurate, it serves as an emblem of the perilous state of revolutionary hopes at the end of 1907. Fearing police surveillance at the railway station and main port, Lenin decided to board a steamer to Stockholm from a small island where the boat made a scheduled stop. The island could be reached by walking across ice but the journey there did not go according to plan and Lenin found himself relying on a pair of apparently inebriated peasants to show him the way. At one stage, the ice began to move under their feet and, according to Krupskaya, he thought: *Oh, what a silly way to have to die*.[49] Lenin survived, however, and made it safely to Stockholm, then on to Geneva for a few months before settling in Paris at the end of 1908.

The events of 1905 in Russia had caused Lenin to reflect on and change the authoritarian, centralist ideas of *What Is To Be Done?* and its espousal of an elitist group of professional revolutionaries. During the period when the government found itself forced to liberalise its rule, party membership had soared, from less than 9,000 in January 1905 to over 70,000 by October 1906. Soon after his return to St Petersburg from exile Lenin began to call for a more open party and a level of democratic centralism, based on elections and the involvement of the mass of party members, that had not been contemplated in *What Is To Be Done?*. He acknowledged that the Moscow insurrection showed workers moving forward from a strike to an uprising without being instructed to do so by a party leadership. He also came to realise the significance of the soviets, which had emerged outside of the party, as embryonic workers' governments. Such flexibility, an ability to combine, somewhat paradoxically, a sense of doctrinal purity with a keen pragmatism, becomes a characteristic feature of his approach: hence his criticism of Mensheviks in 1905 for being *afraid of losing the book knowledge they have learned by rote (but not assimilated).*[50]

Events on the ground focused Lenin's attention on the need for a decisive rupture with the Mensheviks; and the battleground centred around the question of political alliance with liberal opposition to the Tsar. The events of 1905–6 convinced Lenin that liberals could not be trusted, that at a crucial stage they would ally themselves with reactionary forces; for Mensheviks, though, the value of seeking an alliance with the Kadets was confirmed by what had happened in Russia following Bloody Sunday. Behind this difference lay a fundamental divergence of opinion towards parliamentary politics. Mensheviks could see themselves working constitutionally within a Duma, as part of a long-term strategy while for Lenin any support given to the Duma was only a tactic, a way of furthering a revolutionary consciousness that would do away with an institution that could not implement a revolution from below. What was more important, Lenin stressed, was an alliance between workers and peasants, one that could create structures of self-government and its own organs of authority. He drew on the example of the soviets to show how this had begun to happen in the revolutionary ferment of 1905 and how it was essentially a democratic process. The soviets could only function, he argued, if they had the support of the people and involved them in the process of government. This was all well and good but Lenin did not dwell on the complex issues behind the merging of such ideas alongside a highly centralised Bolshevik party.

With the defeat of the revolutionary forces in Russia, the blossoming of Lenin's thought on party matters came to an abrupt end. Political activism was crushed, party membership plummeted and the situation was dire: a *period of absolute stagnation, of dead calm, hangings and suicides, of the orgy of reaction.*[51] Lenin retreated to the idea of a centralised, tightly organised party as doctrinal differences between Bolsheviks and Mensheviks became sectarian. There were also divisions within Bolshevism and Lenin set out to attack and ostracise Bogdanov, seeing him as a threat to his authority and the purity of the party. Lenin, anxious to preserve the party's identity at a time of severe demoralisation, was merciless in attacking anyone or any group that in his eyes threatened the party's integrity. With this in mind he set about a criticism of Bogdanov's philosophy, fearing its intellectualism would encourage the kind of reformism that Lenin labelled opportunism.

Bogdanov, whose real name was Alexander Malinovsky (1873–1928), graduated with a medical degree and, after reading Lenin's *What Is To Be Done?*, became a founder-member of the Bolshevik group. An important and valuable ally of Lenin from 1904 – he led the Bolshevik section in the St Petersburg soviet during the 1905 revolution – differences of opinion and increasing criticism from Lenin led to an irrevocable break in 1909. Withdrawing from active politics, he wrote a number of influential texts on social and cultural matters, including a science fiction novel *Red Star: The First Bolshevik Utopia*. After 1917, Bogdanov became involved in radical, communist-inspired cultural projects. His understanding of philosophical issues left Lenin far behind and as an original and exciting thinker he continued to be regarded with suspicion. He was arrested by the authorities in 1923 but released after questioning and five years later, as a result of his involvement in blood transfusion experiments, he died in an accident. It is doubtful if he would have survived Stalin's purges.

While Lenin's assault on Bogdanov took the form of an attack on his philosophical position, his underlying intention was to undermine someone capable of changing the focus of the Bolsheviks. Bogdanov advocated a withdrawal from the Duma in order to concentrate on the rebuilding of an underground party within Russia and, complementing this, the opening-up of a cultural front that would help advance the process of liberation. Bogdanov argued for the need to create a 'proletarian culture', one where working people could think and create outside the box of bourgeois habits of thought, challenging notions of individualism and submission to authority. Although he did not focus on the area of sexuality, Bogdanov anticipated the ideas of another radical communist, Wilhelm Reich, in drawing attention to the limitations of a narrowly political, 'purist' approach to the task of changing society. There was an originality and intellectual daring about Bogdanov that gained him the support of fellow Bolsheviks as well as influential supporters like Gorky; Lenin set about the task of demolishing his rival's credentials.

In May 1908, Lenin left Geneva for London in order to work at the British Library and took a flat at 21 Tavistock Place. He immersed himself in philosophical literature in order to demonstrate what he saw as the misguided and reactionary nature of Bogdanov's thought. The result was *Materialism and Empiriocriticism*, published in 1909, a book that relies philosophically more on Engels than Marx. Most ironically, Lenin criticises a thinker like Bogdanov for departing from Marxism when in fact it is Lenin himself who reveals a partial understanding of Marxist philosophy. In fairness to Lenin, the writings of Marx now recognised as central to his philosophical radicalism were not available at the time he was writing and this needs to be borne in mind. *Critique of Hegel's Philosophy of Right* was not published until 1927 and it was 1932 before the full text of *The German Ideology* was published, the same year that the text of *Economic and Philosophical Manuscripts* came to light. It remains the case, though, that Bogdanov was far closer to Marx when he advanced ideas about the relationship between consciousness and reality that Lenin stridently denounced as revisionist.

Lenin uses the 18th-century philosopher George Berkeley as a cudgel with which to beat Bogdanov, charging him with being a reactionary idealist. He insists that Bogdanov is like Berkeley in denying the fundamental reality of the material world and our cognition of the physical components of this reality. For Lenin, this is the bedrock of Marxist materialism and he quotes Engels to support his claim that our knowledge of the world is a direct reflection of the way things really are in the physical world. Bogdanov is a heretic because his epistemology does not endorse the materialism of Engels. Unfortunately, Engels had not engaged with Hegel in the way that Marx did; and Lenin, like Plekhanov and many others, accepted as orthodox an epistemology that was rather simplistic.

Bishop Berkeley (1685–1763), seeking to rebut what he saw as the dangerous scepticism and mechanistic materialism of his age, advanced the startling claim that matter did not exist. In doing so he was challenging the view that material reality affects the sense-organs of human beings and by operating through the brain causes ideas to arise in the mind.[52] Berkeley argued that if our knowledge of reality depends ultimately on ideas in the mind how do we have a sure way of knowing that there is a reality outside of our mind? By denying matter altogether and arguing that our ideas come from God, Berkeley wished to defend the veracity and coherence of what we do experience and prevent the development of a godless materialism. He advances his strikingly original and extraordinary position with a dazzling ingenuity, capable of confounding many an argument designed to show its absurdity, but Lenin does not dwell on this.

Marx's *Theses on Feuerbach*, which was available to Lenin and which was studied by Bogdanov, advances a radically different understanding of materialism. Indeed, it criticises the very kind of reductionist thinking that Lenin is championing. For Marx there is not a given world that is simply there, independent of our existence. The philosophical investigation of what there is, ontology, does not lead to a simple relationship between the subject, the 'I', and the object, the world that seems to exist independently of the 'I'. Instead, there is a dynamic relationship whereby it is we ourselves, our praxis and our consciousness, that account for and change reality.[53] Marx is not falling into an anti-realist or idealist position because a material reality is not being denied; reality is there but it is always and utterly our creation, and therefore available to change at every level.

For Marx, it makes little sense to think of reality as something simply existing outside of the knowing subject. It is through human practice, the way we produce and what we produce, and the way we express ourselves that humanity constitutes itself and its world. Hegel gave Marx the idea of the dialectic as the dynamic interaction between subject and object but Marx, by giving history an ontological identity, makes history and not consciousness the very being of reality. This is not idealism but it does, by making the mind a transformative force within reality and not a reflection of it, deny the objective existence of things and ideas. Everything that exists, from genes to jeans, did not, in a literal as well as a philosophical sense, exist until it came to be known. What does come to be known, the result of collective human practice, has an objective existence.

It was Bogdanov's understanding of a Marxist ontology, quite remarkable at a time when so much of what Marx had written on this topic was unavailable, that gave his thought a complexity that was at odds with what Lenin took to be Marxism. Bogdanov seemed to be denying the notion of absolute truth in a way that Lenin saw as robbing cognition of its ability to take a grip on the world. It was a simple choice for Lenin between a Marxist materialism and a Berkeley-like idealism: either reality was the object, with the subject registering and reflecting its material existence in the human consciousness, or there was no material reality and only ideas in the mind. Lenin demanded an understanding of reality that was as incontrovertible as the rules that governed the grammar of the Latin and Greek he had learned at school in Simbirsk. Bogdanov was interested in breaking down the simple dualism of a subject–object epistemology and replacing it with a view of reality, in terms of socially organised experience, that he had gained from *Theses on Feuerbach* and elsewhere in Marx. He was interested in ideas of cognitive psychology associated with philosophers of science like Ernst Mach and Richard Avenarius and, given the relativity of forms of knowledge, the importance of developing non-bourgeois concepts of experience and culture. This was academic twaddle to Lenin, a distraction that could dilute the task in hand, especially when some of Bogdanov's supporters espoused socialism as a new and better of kind of religion, and he denounced Bogdanov as a 'God-builder' and a puppet of Mach's 'empiriocriticism'. At a meeting of leading Bolsheviks in Paris in June 1909, Lenin succeeded in marginalising Bogdanov for good.

Much of 1908 had been taken up with *Materialism and Empiriocriticism* and establishing a new home, first in Geneva and then Paris. He kept in regular contact with his sisters and his mother, concerned with a bout of illness suffered by Maria and wondering whether he was overwhelming her with requests for books and minutes of the Third Duma. By October, with his book completed, he was hoping that Anna could find a publisher and explained to her that securing good royalties was less important than getting it quickly into print. By April 1909, he was anxious to use the book against Bogdanov at the Bolshevik meeting coming up in June. *I have not only literary but also serious political commitments that are linked up with the publication of the book.*[54] As ever, though, he was conscientious about accuracy and handled the need for meticulous proofreading with exemplary proficiency.

So much of what is known about Lenin concerns the

contours of his political, consciously active self and so little
about areas that he chose not to reveal that it is often difficult to trace how his more personal self was developing.
Before the end of 1908, Maria had come to stay with him
and Krupskaya in Geneva and she moved with them to Paris.
Maria, pursuing her education overseas and requiring hospital treatment, stayed with them until the autumn of 1909.
Krupskaya's elderly mother, who had been with them in
Kuokkala, also made the move from Geneva to Paris. Lenin's
own mother became ill early in 1909 and he was reassured to
hear from his brother Dmitri, a doctor, that she was making
a full recovery. After the long bout of disagreement with
Bogdanov, Lenin himself was feeling the strain and in August
1909, with Krupskaya and Maria, he took a six-week holiday
outside of Paris. He took another holiday with them the following year and in September organised a family reunion in
Stockholm with his mother and Maria. It was to be the last
time he saw his mother and Krupskaya remembered how mel-
ancholy he felt as he waved goodbye to her on the departing
steamer from Stockholm. These personal contacts with his
family were very important to Lenin and seem to have been as
vital to his well being as the outdoor holidays when he could
walk, cycle, swim and relax in the countryside. There was
far more to Lenin's chemistry than allowed for in the stere-
otype of the obsessive revolutionary but much of it remains
inaccessible to others because this is how he wanted it to be.
Outside of politics, Lenin was not given to the talking cure
and the dictum of Chernyshevsky that he approved of, about
everyone's need for a private corner in their life, remained a
constant of his own existence. He guarded his privacy, just
as he respected the private lives of others, and was loath to
drop his defences when people tried to pry into the state of

his feelings or his character. When Nikolai Valentinov, who knew him in Geneva before 1905, pressed for such details he was rebuffed: *There's no need for all that.*[55] Such a protective shield encouraged others to think that his political activities constituted the only window into his soul and this encouraged the caricature of Lenin as a ruthless and cynical personality, inhumanly dedicated to achieving his objectives. The writer Maxim Gorky was able to sense unspoken depths below the surface that point to a more complex individual: 'He could give to his short characteristic exclamation, "H'm, h'm" an infinite number of modifications ... one caught the sound of the keen humour which a sharp-sighted man experiences who sees clearly through the stupidities of life.'[56]

The difficulty of tracing developments in Lenin's personal life, the difficulty of knowing him, is epitomised by the uncertainty surrounding the nature of his relationship with Inessa Armand and how this relationship affected his marriage. While there is no sure proof that Lenin and Inessa were lovers – though this has not prevented one unrevealing biography of Inessa being entitled *Lenin's Mistress*[57] – it does seem likely.

Inessa Armand was born in Paris in 1891 but following the failure of her parents' marriage she was taken to Russia as a child by her aunt and grandmother. She married Alexander Armand and had five children but left him for his brother, Vladimir, through whom she became involved in revolutionary politics. She was exiled to just below the Arctic Circle in 1907 but escaped at the end of 1908 and made it to France, just in time to be reunited with Vladimir who was dying of TB. After his death, she settled in the Russian émigré circle in Paris with her two youngest children and it was here, aged 35, that she met Lenin in 1909 and became involved in Bolshevik activities.

Lenin and Inessa became very close, and in the autumn of 1911 she moved in next-door to him in Paris. There was, however, nothing secretive about their enjoyment of each other's company and, according to Alexandra Kollontai, Krupskaya offered to leave but Lenin refused to break up their marriage. There is no certainty about how the relationship affected Krupskaya but it is clear that Inessa also endeared herself to Krupskaya and in time the two of them became good friends.

What is known with more certainty is that these were trying years for Lenin. He was approaching his forties, a political exile still quarrelling with fellow revolutionaries and trying to assert his interpretation of Marxism and what needed to be done. The Russian Social Democrat party was riddled with factions – there were ten different factions by 1914 – and Lenin was far from being even an undisputed leader of the Bolsheviks. He was hardly known inside Russia, and had to endure the prickly micropolitics and petty squabbling that characterised Russian émigré circles: *Life in exile is now a hundred times harder than it was before the revolution.*[58] There were frequent short trips to European cities to deliver talks and attend meetings but Paris was wearing him down. By 1912 there were signs of renewed activism in his home country and the Bolshevik organisation was shifting its base there as well.

Alexandra Mikhaylovna Kollontai (1872–1952) was a Russian revolutionary who stayed in the Menshevik camp until finally committing herself to the Bolsheviks in 1914. When the First World War broke out she was in Germany and witnessed the Social Democrats in the Reichstag voting for hostilities. She was so shocked, she wrote afterwards, that she thought she might be going mad. She welcomed Lenin's position, rallied to his side and was one of the very few to support him when he opposed the rest of the party. She got to know Inessa Armand in post-revolution Russia and her novella, *The Great Love*, was published there in 1927. It is a fictionalised account of the Lenin–Inessa–Krupskaya triangle.

Lenin decided to move eastwards, settling a few miles from the frontier in the city of Kraków, then in Austrian Galicia but *Almost in Russia! ... the women go barefoot and wear brightly-coloured clothes, exactly as in Russia.*[59] He felt better, the summers of 1913 and 1914 being spent enjoyably in the countryside, but Krupskaya was suffering from a thyroid complaint that had plagued her for years and he arranged for her to have an operation in Switzerland. Inessa spent time with them in the Galician countryside but, based on a letter Inessa wrote to him from Paris, it seems that around this time Lenin called a halt to the passionate aspect of their relationship. She wrote: 'When I gaze at these places I know so well, I realise more clearly than ever how big a place you occupied in my life here in Paris, so that almost all activity has been bound by a thousand threads to my thoughts of you ... . Even here I could cope without your kisses if only I could see you. To talk with you sometimes would be such a joy for me – and this could not cause pain to anyone. Why deprive me of that? You asked me if I am angry with you for "carrying through" our separation. No, for I don't think that it was for your sake that you did it.'[60] They remained friends, however, politically as well as personally.

Lenin had been reading Tolstoy's *War and Peace* while on holiday in Galicia but it could hardly have prepared him for responding to the very real conflagration that flared when the First World War broke out in August 1914. It was not the war itself that came as a shock to Lenin – war had been a constant topic of conversation for the past decade – but the response to it from the European left. To his disbelief when he first heard the news, the Social Democrats in Germany, the largest and most influential socialist party in the world, unanimously supported the hostilities;[61] their response was followed by like-minded resolutions from Social Democrat parties across Europe. The anti-war resolution that the Second International had passed in Stuttgart in 1907 counted for nothing. It was only in Serbia that the two socialist deputies opposed what was happening, while in the Russian Duma Mensheviks and Bolsheviks united temporarily but could only abstain from the vote supporting the war. Lenin, initially arrested by the authorities of a government at war with Russia, was released when his opposition to Tsarism was established and in September he and Krupskaya quickly left for neutral Switzerland. The Second International had died, even Plekhanov supported the call to arms, and the ideals of the socialist movement floundered amidst a potent mix of patriotism, nationalism and war fever. It was a difficult time to stand apart from the crowd but Lenin, to his credit, did just that and his controversial position won him the respect of non-Bolsheviks like Trotsky and Kollontai.

At a conference of concerned socialists organised at Zimmerwald in Switzerland in the autumn of 1915 – fewer than 40 delegates were able to attend – Lenin found himself largely isolated in his call for revolutionary defeatism. He argued that the working classes of Europe should be at war with their governments, not each other, and Russia's defeat by Germany should be welcomed as it would hasten a revolution. Many

The First World War saw Germany, Austria-Hungary and Turkey ranged against France, Belgium, Russia, Britain and Serbia. Other countries – Japan, the US and China – later joined the alliance against Germany. What was expected to be a short war dragged on for four years after the German advance was forced to retreat at the Battle of the Marne and the Russian incursion into German territory halted at the Battles of Tannenberg and Masurian Lakes. In the earlier war with Japan, defeat for Russia had been mitigated by the favourable terms of the Treaty of Portsmouth in August 1905; this time, no peace treaty was on the horizon and the Russian people turned against their government.

comrades found this hard to swallow but Lenin stood his ground. Contact with the homeland was difficult and Bolshevik groups in Petrograd (St Petersburg's new, less German-sounding name) had been arrested; news of Lenin's principled stand only slowly became known in Russia. State repression there was effective in breaking up the Bolshevik organisation and one consequence of this was an unexpected squeeze on Lenin's finances. He was no longer being regularly paid by the party and money was in short supply in the Lenin household. Economies needed to be made: they moved into cheaper accommodation and Lenin came to increasingly rely on payments for articles.

Lenin's years in Switzerland, first in Berne and then in Zurich, were strange times and for very different reasons they have attracted the interest of Alexander Solzhenitsyn and Tom Stoppard.[62] The Russian novelist projects Lenin as intensely mistrustful and febrile, driven by a demon to relentlessly plot and politicise, while Stoppard's play is a more light-hearted affair, conjuring a trilogy of contrasting, revolutionary intellects out of the fact that Lenin, Tristan Tzara and James Joyce were resident in Zurich in 1917 and could have met one another. Krupskaya's non-fictional account of their time in Zurich has its own surreal touches: the soon-to-be leader of Russia lodging at first with the lumpenproletariat and enjoying his mealtimes with a criminal and a prostitute in an intelligent atmosphere where 'there was more of the human, the living element, than that heard in the prim dining rooms of a respectable hotel patronised by well-to-do guests'.[63]

Stoppard sets much of his play in a library, which is apposite given that the city's public library was the attraction for Lenin coming to Zurich in February 1916. He had begun to read Hegel in September 1914, making notes on his *The*

Science of Logic, and his studies continued in Zurich. His reading of Marx's *Theses on Feuerbach* exposed the crudity of his earlier understanding of materialism and he must have realised that Bogdanov was far from being the hopelessly misguided revisionist that he had made him out to be. In his notes, Lenin acknowledged the limitations of a vulgar materialism, *its inability to apply dialectics to the theory of reflection, to the process and development of knowledge*, and admitted that philosophical idealism was not pure nonsense but a *one-sided, exaggerated, development* of *one of the features, aspects, facets of knowledge* that only became nonsensical when *divorced from matter, from nature*.[64] This more complex and exciting understanding of Hegel and Marx deepened Lenin's intuitive grasp of history's dynamic and the fundamentally changeable nature of reality. The Lenin of *Materialism and Empiriocriticism* had clung to a static epistemology that inhibited the author's natural talent for recognising and responding to the contingent. A dialectical materialism made everything possible in the whoosh of history, allowing for February 1917 to be somersaulted in an audacious leap towards the authentic Revolution. Orthodox pieties about necessary stages of historical development and the need for a bourgeois revolution before a proletarian one could be abandoned when a unique opportunity presented itself.[65]

When not reading Hegel there were other matters of concern to Lenin, for as well as money worries there were personal setbacks to be borne. In March 1915, Krupskaya's mother died and in the following summer came news of the death of his own mother. She had been one of the constants in his life and now he could not even attend her funeral in Petrograd. The personal life of Lenin and Krupskaya was also affected by Inessa's return. She had left Kraków at the end of

1913 and moved to Paris but in September 1914 she arrived in Berne and lived across the street from them. Krupskaya, describing one of the excursions they often took together into the countryside, evokes a happy threesome: with Lenin making notes for an article, Krupskaya learning Italian from a book and Inessa sewing a skirt, 'we would sit for hours on the sunlit-wooded mountainside'.[66] If there was a renewal of amorous relations between Lenin and Inessa – though there is no evidence for this – Krupskaya was either unaware, indifferent or in denial. Inessa left for Paris at the start of 1916 and she only saw him once more before they shared passage in the infamous 'sealed' train that took them to Russia. When Inessa was away from Switzerland, Lenin wrote regularly to her and when there was no news from her, Lenin fretfully enquired: *Don't you feel lonely? Are you very busy? You are causing me great anxiety by not giving any news about yourself! ... Where are you living? Where do you eat?*[67]

Lenin was also working hard to win support for his opposition to the war and worrying about the backsliding of former comrades who could not see the need for an internationalist perspective. It stimulated him into thinking about colonialism and capitalism. The result was the prescient *Imperialism: The Highest Stage of Capitalism*, foreseeing globalisation by its focus on the stage of capitalism characterised by the export of capital. The commerce of commodity production, formerly the typical feature of capitalist development, has been changed *by the entry of numerous backward countries into international capitalist intercourse.*[68] In its preliminary stage this takes the form of the kind of territorial ownership that characterised the 'scramble for Africa' and, anticipating the cause of the Second World War in Asia, he observes that the rivalry between the US and Japan over China is just beginning.

Lenin goes beyond this stage of territorial penetration and discerns the process of imperialism extending ownership by means of finance capital and reaching *states enjoying complete political independence.*[69] The monopolist concentration of capital in the hands of a few does not replace free competition but *hovers over it*[70] and gives rise to its own conflicts and frictions. For Lenin, the uneven and changing developments between the competitive wielders of capital provide the starting point for explaining the economic foundation of imperialist wars. Previous scholarship on the nature of imperialism[71] provided Lenin with a lot of the ground he was covering but part of the cutting edge that he brought to the analysis arose from the explanatory power he gave it in the context of the First World War. For Lenin, the underlying cause of the slaughter on the battlefields was rival imperialisms and history was bearing him out. Germany, lacking the colonial possessions of Britain, wanted the iron-ore region of France, hegemony in central Europe and influence in Turkey and the Middle East; and the treaties of Brest-Litovsk and Versailles revealed the economic plunder that awaited the stronger powers.

> When the profit motive focuses on the most suitable place of production, sometimes hundreds or thousands of miles away ... right up to the manufacture of numerous varieties of finished articles; when these products are distributed according to a single plan among tens of hundreds of millions of consumers ... private economic relations and private property relations constitute a shell which is no longer suitable for its contents ...
>
> Lenin on globalisation[72]

At the Zimmerwald conference Lenin's attitude towards the war, calling for a revolutionary civil war in place of the imperialist one, had not won majority support and the same was the case at another conference in Kienthal, again in Switzerland, in April 1916. Unlike previous occasions when he was at odds with fellow Marxists, Lenin was not unduly stressed by the differences of opinion and afterwards he and Krupskaya enjoyed a six-week summer break in the mountains. When they left their lodgings, other guests sang 'Good-bye, cuckoo' as a farewell and they missed the train home because Lenin insisted on collecting mushrooms spotted on the road to the station.

The sanguine mood lasted through to the following year and then astonishing news from Russia shattered the calm. A revolution had broken out, the Tsar had abdicated and a self-appointed Provisional Government had assumed power until a democratic Constituent Assembly decided on the country's future. In Zurich, Lenin had just finished dinner when a friend rushed in to the house and delivered the news. This time, unlike 1905, there would be no dallying on the sidelines and the only problem was how Lenin and fellow Bolsheviks could reach Russia. Discussions took place through Fritz Platten, a Swiss Social Democrat, with the German ambassador and plans were agreed for émigrés to return through Germany to Sweden and then on to Finland and Petrograd. Towards the end of March, in a group of 32 that included Krupskaya and Inessa, he boarded a train for the start of the journey home.

Legend has it that Lenin and his comrades travelled to Russia in a hermetically-sealed train – Churchill famously likened the conveyance to 'a plague bacillus and more deadly than any bomb' – but the truth is less dramatic. Well aware of being labelled traitors by the Provisional Government, Lenin insisted they pay their own fares, not leave the train at any stage of the journey, and that Fritz Platten would accompany them and act as go-between with the German authorities. A carriage was reserved for the Russian emigrants, off-limits to all but Platten and while three of the four doors were closed there was open access into an adjoining German officers' carriage. At Frankfurt station, some soldiers and railway workers used this to board and chat to the Bolsheviks.

At Stockholm the group took sledges across the border to Finland and boarded a slow train for Petrograd. Apart from the short stay in 1905–6, Lenin had spent the previous 17 years in exile; now, aged 46, the Leninist moment was fast approaching.

Lenin in disguise for his escape to Finland in July 1917.

The Leninist Moment

The First World War was a disaster for Russia, with some five million causalities by 1917, and it helped bring about the end of the tottering autocracy that ruled with increasing incompetence over a deeply divided society. Towards the end of February 1917, shortages of bread led to strikes and demonstrations in Petrograd and with troops fraternising with protestors it became clear that something had to give.

No one had planned the February revolution, it was a spontaneous revolt from below, precipitated by a women's strike on International Women's Day, and the crucial factor was the refusal by troops to open fire on unarmed crowds in Petrograd. The dominant class of army leaders, Duma politicians, industrialists and aristocrats quickly turned against the Tsar when it seemed clear that this was the best way to restore order and wield power. The Tsar, who was outside the capital at the time, was met on his return journey by emissaries from military and political leaders and he agreed to abdicate. A Provisional Government, speedily recognised by the Allied powers, was headed by a moderate liberal, Prince Lvov, and a cabinet of leading industrialists, the Kadet politician Pavel Milyukov and the socialist lawyer Alexander Kerensky. The transfer of power to the bourgeoisie, though, was not going to be as seamless an affair as the downfall of Tsarism. The soviet that had first emerged in the capital in 1905 was revived and the Petrograd Soviet of 1917, composed of workers and soldiers, was a volatile grouping though with a moderate, informal leadership. In this way, a system of dual power emerged between the Provisional Government and the mostly Menshevik members of the Executive Committee of the Soviet. The self-important Kerensky acted as the go-between.

Stalin (1879–1953) was born in Georgia, the son of a cobbler, and trained as a priest before his skills as an organiser were recognised in the struggle against Tsarism. He flourished when the 1905 revolution turned the Caucasus into a lawless state and he created the first Bolshevik partisans. By robbing banks they brought in valuable funds for the party and this was how he first came to the attention of Lenin. He played an active role in the October revolution and in 1922 became General Secretary of the Bolshevik party. After Lenin's death he gradually isolated his political rivals and became virtual dictator of the USSR.

Kerensky had the task of trying to reconcile conflicting views about Russia's continuing role in the War. The Provisional Government was determined to maintain the war effort while grass-roots feeling in the soviets that had sprung up, reflecting the general mood of the country, wanted an end to hostilities and the return of troops from the Front. The first Bolsheviks to return to Petrograd, those who had been arrested and exiled after 1914 for opposing Russia's participation in the war, were hovering on the edge of joining the Mensheviks and Socialist-Revolutionaries (SRs) who supported the Provisional Government. They began rebuilding the Bolshevik party and re-establishing the party newspaper, *Pravda*, which from mid-March included J V Stalin on its editorial board.

Lenin received a warm welcome when he arrived at Petrograd's Finland Station on the night of 3 April and Eisenstein's

October accurately recreates the drama, including the speech he made from atop an armoured car outside the station. The film, though, does not dwell on the shocked reaction of those who heard him immediately denounce the Provisional Government. From the station he went on to deliver the same message at the Bolshevik headquarters in the early hours of 4 April, at the expropriated luxury mansion of the ballerina Matilda Kseshinskaya, who had been Tsar Nicholas's mistress. Its luxury (silk-covered walls, velvet curtains, ormolu-inlaid couches and a modernist bathroom in white marble with a sunken bath) contrasted vividly with his temporary abode in the cramped apartment where his sister Anna, her husband Mark and their adopted son were staying. Maria Ulyanov was also staying here but room was found for Lenin and Krupskaya.[73] His first night's sleep back in Russia was a very short one for he was up for breakfast and then a journey to the cemetery to pay his respects at the graves of his mother and sister Olga. From the cemetery he travelled to the Tauride Palace – the Petrograd Soviet and the Provisional Government having taken over the former home of the Duma – and again declared his position to Bolsheviks from across Russia.

Lenin's views had first been expressed in his *Letters from Afar*, written before he left Switzerland, and the first two were brought to Petrograd by Alexandra Kollontai on 19 March. They are astonishingly lucid documents, shot through with a burning red light that illuminates the post-February situation. The first of them appeared in *Pravda* – the three other letters (the fifth was unfinished) were not published in 1917 – but edited to tone down his attack on the Mensheviks and the SRs. In this first letter, Lenin's incisive analysis goes to the heart of the matter: the revolution is the result of a unique merging of contradictory interests and there can be no common ground between them now that Tsarism is gone. The workers revolted *for freedom, land for the peasants, and for peace, against the imperialist slaughter* and the new government, having seized power in order to continue the slaughter, represents *the class of capitalist landlords and bourgeoisie which has long been ruling our country economically*.[74] The interests of workers and peasants lay with the soviet and he drums home the message that the present situation is only a transitional one. There is unfinished business, the opportunity has presented itself, and workers must prepare for the next stage of the revolution. Lenin was correct in suspecting that many in the Provisional Government would like to restore the monarchy with a new Tsar; it was only the lack of a candidate and popular opposition that prevented this from happening. He was also correct in asserting that the Provisional Government was there to ensure that the country remained in the war.

It was 'The Tasks of the Proletariat in the Present Revolution', better known as the *April Theses* and read by Lenin at two meetings on 4 April before appearing in Bolshevik newspapers across Russia, that spread his uncompromising but not yet insurrectionary message. It caused consternation amongst most Bolsheviks, for whom support for the non-Tsarist Provisional Government, the result of a popular revolution after all, seemed reasonable in the circumstances. Was it not sensible to consolidate what had been gained by the overthrow of Tsarism in February? Lenin denounced this position. Russia's participation in a *predatory imperialist war*[75] should cease and he called instead for a class war that would expropriate the landed estates, tear down the existing machinery of state power – the police, army and bureaucracy – and transfer all power to the soviets. Bakunin would have applauded and it is not surprising that many Russian anarchists were won over by Lenin's stance; but the majority of Bolsheviks who listened to him on 4 April at the Tauride Palace would need more convincing. They thought he was being premature and reckless, if not downright cranky, and a few days later the board of *Pravda* dissociated itself and the party from his *April Theses*. Bogdanov, still supporting the Bolsheviks after returning from the Front where he had served as a doctor, was not alone in thinking his old adversary had lost the plot. This, though, was the Leninist moment: virtually alone, he dared to imagine and promote the idea of a second revolution; not history repeating itself but, by seizing possibilities in the pregnant space created by the events of February, changing the form and not just the content of revolution. No longer the library-bound armchair revolutionary, Lenin was on his feet and reinventing the Bolshevik party.

Lenin's achievement between April and October is all the more remarkable given the nature of the Bolshevik party and his initial isolation within it. At the time, the party was not a smooth, monolithic machine with switches and gears to be operated by whoever was in charge. There were factions and competing points of view and no single individual was capable of dictating policy. Some Bolsheviks and Mensheviks still hoped to unite as a party but when Lenin addressed a third meeting on 4 April, this time a mixed audience of socialists, his polemic drew a line in the sand and made absolute the separate identity of Bolshevism. Within the country as a whole, Lenin's party was by no means in the ascendancy. At a national congress of soviets in June, where only 105 of the 822 delegates were Bolsheviks, SRs and Mensheviks predominated.

After February, Russia had suddenly become a remarkably

free state and the removal of many forms of censorship, psychological and legal, created an extraordinary fluidity of thought and action. Anarchists had a popular following but there were also parties agitating for a non-socialist state – the bourgeoisie came to rely increasingly on the Kadet party – and the wealthy, propertied class was anxious to preserve its way of life. In Petrograd, cocktails were still being served in Hotel Europe by a noted bartender from New York's Waldorf-Astoria and Tamara Karsavina could still be seen on the stage.[76] Krupskaya recalled how, walking down Nevsky Prospect in late April, she encountered a workers' march and 'another crowd wearing hats and bowlers ... "Kill all these scoundrels," shouted a stylishly dressed girl.'[77] She also heard working people damning her husband as a German spy and traitor. The democratic election of a Constituent Assembly would take months to organise and in the meantime Lenin worked to create a Bolshevik mentality with enough popular support to warrant an utterly new kind of government.

April turned Lenin into a politician. He made speeches, wrote for *Pravda*, argued and listened, honed his vocabulary and rallying calls and tried to keep abreast of events outside of the capital; alert and cautious to the danger of precipitate action that reactionary forces could exploit. He was virtually unknown within Russia when he had arrived at the Finland Station but his name was becoming a familiar presence in *Pravda*. The clarity of thought and militant logic that is such a defining feature of the *April Theses* found expression in his newspaper articles just as it did in his public speeches. Short and stocky, dressed in a suit but with a workaday cap, his energy and excitement overcame the fact that he was not a naturally gifted speaker.

Lenin gained credibility when it became known on 18 April

that the Foreign Minister, Milyukov, had informed the Allies that Russia still planned to annex Ottoman territory. At a Bolshevik conference, starting on 24 April, Lenin overcame the criticisms of Lev Kamenev by acknowledging the need to build up support in the country as a whole. A Central Committee for the party was elected – Lenin received the highest number of votes – adding a third element to the Bolshevik organisation. Since March the party's Military Organisation had been in existence, representing Bolshevik soldiers and sailors, and there was also the Petrograd Committee charged with coordinating party activities in the capital. Early in May, Trotsky arrived from America and Lenin invited him to join the Bolsheviks. In early June, when a planned anti-government demonstration threatened to turn into armed conflict, Lenin counselled moderation and went along with the soviets' leadership who opposed the march. Lenin warmed to the mood of militancy but also sensed the danger of adventurist, premature action giving the government an excuse to suppress the Bolsheviks.

Lev Borisovich Kamenev (1883–1936) joined the Russian revolutionary movement in 1901 and was exiled to Siberia in 1915. Released after the February revolution he became a member of the Bolshevik's Central Committee. After Lenin's death he was expelled from the party by Stalin and denounced as a Trotskyist. He was readmitted in 1928 but expelled again in 1932 and later shot in Moscow for allegedly conspiring against Stalin.

Though initially lacking the support of most Bolsheviks, Lenin became increasingly in step with the developing mood of the country. Thousands of workers were joining the party and, with army desertions increasing, there was growing dissatisfaction with the failure of the government to end the war or improve the economic situation. Militancy was growing in the soviets, as shown by 'Order No. 1 to the Petrograd

Garrison', issued by the Petrograd Soviet on 1 March. In a revolutionary spirit of democracy it called for the election of soldiers' committees in the Army and insisted that any government order to the Army required the approval of the Soviet before it could be considered valid. In some units soldiers and sailors began implementing democratic procedures, forcibly removing officers regarded as enemies of the revolution, and workers' committees had taken over management of production in the factories. Landowners were fleeing from their estates as the revolutionary temper spread to the countryside; peasants demanded all the land their families had worked as serfs and, starting in the summer, began seizing land. What was happening contradicts historians like Richard Pipes ('people do not make history – they make a living'[78]) who tend to believe that popular experience is not a telling factor in shaping history. The radicalism of the sailors at the Kronstadt naval base, close to Petrograd, was never in doubt – anarchists and Bolsheviks worked together in its soviet – and in the working-class Vyborg district of the capital, where huge factories employed thousands, support for Lenin was growing solid. Here too was stationed the First Machine-Gun Regiment, 10,000 politicised soldiers who had mutinied in February and distrusted the Provisional Government. The truth of Lenin's unceasing message, that the government was doing nothing to stop the war or change Russia's class system, was becoming increasingly clear. His insistence that ownership of the means of production should be in the hands of workers and peasants was striking home.

In May, representatives of the Mensheviks and SRs joined the government and these socialists were able to use their majority in the Petrograd soviet's Executive Committee and present themselves as 'responsible' leaders. This initially strengthened Kerensky's middle-of-the-road position but the second half of June saw the failure of the first major military operation since February, a new Russian offensive on the Eastern Front that Kerensky had encouraged. On 3 July the First Machine-Gun Regiment decided to resist a government order to leave the city and the size of their march through the city on the following day was swelled by workers and armed sailors from Kronstadt. With more than half a million demonstrators marching through Petrograd calling on the government to resign, there was the possibility of an armed revolt against the government. The mood of insurgency took Bolshevik leaders by surprise and an exhausted Lenin was resting outside of the capital when he was suddenly called back. He addressed a group of the demonstrators but held back from publicly encouraging the openly-insurgent atmosphere. The government held the Bolsheviks responsible for the disorder that followed the march, even though many of its leaders had been reluctant to support the demonstration, and measures were taken to suppress the party and arrest its leaders. Newspapers carried reports of Lenin as a traitor in the pay of the Germans, based on no firm evidence because it did not exist, and his sister's flat was raided in the search for him; Kollontai, Kamenev and others were under arrest and *Pravda's* printing press destroyed. Kerensky became prime minister and moved into the opulent Winter Palace, sleeping now in the Tsar's bed and perhaps contentedly so in the knowledge that the Bolsheviks had been dealt a heavy and perhaps fatal blow.

Lenin's pressing need was to ensure his own safety and survival. On 9 July, he left Petrograd with Grigori Zinoviev and together they travelled to a village east of the capital where they remained in hiding, in a thatched hut near a colleague's house. Lenin borrowed a coat and a different kind of cap to wear for the journey and with his beard shaved off there was little chance of him being recognised. His disguise was further improved, a month later, when a wig was added and in his new appearance he was photographed when forged papers were prepared for his travel on to Finland.[79] Lenin was now the most wanted man in Russia – there was a reward of 200,000 roubles for his arrest – and he had reason to fear for his life from renegade troops and loyalist mobs; Kamenev, when he had been arrested, would have been lynched had not a military commander intervened.[80] Lenin had a variety of addresses in Finland, at one stage staying in the apartment of Helsinki's head of police, a trusted Bolshevik.

Grigori Zinoviev (1883–1936) was a Bolshevik in exile before 1917 and supported Lenin's attitude when World War I broke out in 1914. He returned to St Petersburg with Lenin in April 1917 but opposed the idea of an October revolution. He became a leading party member after the revolution but after Lenin's death his opposition to Stalin led to his expulsion from the party and eventual execution. In 1924, the 'Zinoviev Letter' was published by Britain's Foreign Office. It purported to reveal a Moscow plot to stir up violent revolution and succeeded in bringing to an end the first Labour government of Ramsey MacDonald. The Letter was later revealed to be a forgery.

Safe in Finland, in what would be the last period of productive rest in his life, Lenin had time to envisage how a successful workers' revolution could change the nature of the world. A guiding principle was democracy and *to be a democrat means reckoning in reality with the interests of the majority of the people, not the minority*.[81] A realistic reckoning did not require lateral thinking but the realisation that existing state apparatus – the bourgeois state with its standing army, police and bureaucracy – cannot change the existing class order. When socialists join a government, *even when individuals among them are perfectly honest*, they become *either a useless ornament* or *a sort of lightning conductor to divert the people's indignation from the government.*[82] Lenin had proof of this in the way Social Democrats across Europe were supporting an imperialist war. *Power to the Soviets* who *through their own experience would soon learn how to distribute the land, products and grain properly.*[83] The emergence of the soviets, self-governing administrations based on the place of work or the regiment a soldier belonged to, provided Lenin with an alternative and more viable principle of organisation than that of the parliamentary constituency: 'The reality was the working community, not the isolated individual of liberal economics.'[84] Lenin was responding to the intoxicating pace of events: in the countryside, committees of peasants were reorganising the land; more soldiers were deserting than ever before; and the sheer scale of the politicisation affecting working men and women accounts for the revolutionary confidence expressed in *The State and Revolution.* The state could be overthrown because there were enough people willing it to happen and with the ability and the right to constitute and make real an utterly new organisation of society. The explosive, liberating force of *The State and Revolution,* envisaging a new form of communal politics, arose from the ashes after the self-immolation of the European socialist movement in the patriotic fervour of the First World War.

St Petersburg has a population of about two million. Of these, more than half are between the ages of 15 and 65. Take half – one million. Let us even subtract an entire fourth as physically unfit, etc., taking no part in public service at the present moment for justifiable reasons. There remains 750,000 who, serving in the militia, say, one day in fifteen (and receiving their pay for this time from their employees), would form an army of 50,000. That's the type of 'state' we need![85]

Lenin's notes for *The State and Revolution* had begun in

Switzerland before 1917 and he now used his time in Finland to resume his theoretical work. Any state, he observes, is an *organisation of force* and its *violence* is used by one class to suppress another.[86] A Bolshevik state, a *dictatorship of the proletariat*, will at first be no different in this important respect and its force will be used to suppress the minority of exploiters. It will also be a different kind of state, akin to the Paris Commune of 1871, one that will eventually *wither away* because its repressive features – an army, police and bureaucracy – will be replaced by a radical Athenian-style democratisation that will *smash* the existing political order. The administrative structures of capitalism and places of work will be governed by everyone, the coercive authority of the army and police will be the *armed population*, and with participatory democracy infusing institutional organs of force there will be a progressive end to repressive power. Only a minority, the exploiters, will be suppressed but the presumed consequent, that a people will not repress its equals, was a fatal flaw in Lenin's thinking. So too was the belief that the democratic impulse impelling this new order would eventually allow the ladder of the state to be kicked away: *We do not at all disagree with the anarchists on the question of the abolition of the state as an aim.*

The State and Revolution asserts unashamedly the need to use state power to crush opposition but with an inspirational quality that verges on the visionary when it comes to describing how a proletarian state will be fundamentally different to the Western model of democracy. Such a state, he outlines, will be equally well organised and administered but not in the interests of the few, it will be a communal, *voluntary centralism* and the liberation of the exploited class will benefit everyone because the proletariat is an index of humanity. The role of the party in this process is not highlighted, certainly not the vanguard party of *What Is To Be Done?*, and the emphasis instead is on the self-emancipation of working people. Lenin is again responding to changing circumstances: the Bolshevik party had less than 25,000 members on the eve of the February revolution; by August numbers had catapulted to 200,000. Praxis, not party, was now the issue and it was the need to leave Finland and return to Petrograd in October that brings the text of *The State and Revolution* to an end: *It is more pleasant and useful to go through the 'experience of the revolution' than to write about it.*[87]

The government's response to the so-called 'July Days' almost crushed the Bolsheviks and initially weakened left-wing militancy but a growing sense of frustration at country-wide disorder led right-wing interests to attempt a coup and establish a law-and-order regime. Leading industrialists and military leaders would have welcomed a decisive strike from the right and in August such a move was attempted by General Kornilov, the army's new commander-in-chief. He ordered troops from the front to move on Petrograd but concerted action from railwaymen led to troop trains being diverted and met by workers who persuaded soldiers to question their orders. With a collapse of military morale, the coup attempt petered out and support for the Bolsheviks was renewed. Lenin's party was correctly seen as the only organisation uncontaminated by association with a Provisional Government that was increasingly unable to offer a way forward. To make matters worse, the Germans were advancing and Petrograd was their possible objective.

By the end of August popular discontent was manifesting itself in cities and in the countryside. The formal leadership of the Petrograd Soviet passed into Bolshevik hands – released from prison, Trotsky became its head – and Moscow followed on 5 September. In the first half of September, Lenin called on his party to begin planning for an armed insurrection and the response from most of its leaders was lukewarm at best. Bolshevism had barely survived the July Days and surely, argued erstwhile supporters of Lenin like Zinoviev, it was wiser to wait. Lenin remained isolated but kept up the pressure by writing again, not only to the Central Committee but also to the Bolshevik leaders of the Petrograd and Moscow soviets. He tackled head on the reluctance of the Central Committee to seize power and states unequivocally that it must be overcome: *Otherwise, the Bolsheviks will cover themselves with eternal shame.* Not to act now, he exhorts, would be *treachery* not only to Russian workers and peasants but to the workers of Germany who would be inspired by a Bolshevik revolution. He resigned from the Central Committee, *reserving for myself freedom to campaign among the rank and file of the Party*; if the present moment is allowed to pass *we shall ruin the revolution.*[88] Lenin was still in Finland when this was written, at the end of September, and it was obvious he should be in Petrograd if he meant what he said. He returned on 7 October and continued to call for insurrection from his hiding-place in the Vyborg district. Three days later he attended a Central Committee meeting and won support for his position, with only Kamenev and Zinoviev voting against him. A larger meeting of the party leadership took place on 16 October, including the Military Organisation and the Petrograd Committee, and although Lenin's stand was endorsed, a firm date for insurrection was not established. The following day, Lenin wrote 'Letter to Comrades' dealing with the argument of Kamenev and Zinoviev that the country is not behind the Bolsheviks. They wait for proof that the party has *received exactly one-half of the votes plus one* but this is pedantic: *History has never given such a guarantee.* The fact is that the peasants are in revolt and the workers support Bolshevism: *This is a fact, and facts are stubborn things.*[89]

The insurrection began in Petrograd on 24 October and that evening a heavily disguised Lenin left his hiding-place – with a note for his landlady: *I am going where you did not want me to go. Goodbye. Ilyich*[90] – and, like some of the Irish insurgents of the year before setting off for the Easter Rising, he travelled by bus. Lenin did not know that the revolution had begun until he reached the Bolshevik headquarters at the Smolny Institute. The party's Military Organisation had planned the details and Lenin took no part in directing a takeover of power that at first proceeded like clockwork. Roadblocks were set up, key government buildings occupied and only with the half-bungled siege of the Winter Palace, where the Provisional Government was in session, was blood shed and five people died. The big guns from the Peter and Paul Fortress that were supposed to have bombarded the Winter Palace proved defective and had to be replaced. When the guns were finally ready it was time to signal to the Palace besiegers by raising a red lantern but a lamp was not at hand. Eventually one was found but it was not red and could not be fixed to the flagpole. All this made little difference because the Palace was poorly defended, many soldiers having deserted because there was no food, and even the shot fired at it by the warship *Aurora* on the Neva was a blank.

At 9 a.m. on the morning of 25 October, Kerensky exited history when he slipped out of the Winter Palace in a car hijacked from outside the US Embassy and flying the American flag. Few people noticed him or noted the significance of his departure and it was just another working day for most of those in the city. By late evening of the same day, resistance in the Winter Palace had dwindled away – the Women's Death Battalion defending the Palace did not live up to its fearsome name – and in the early hours of 26 October the remaining members of the Provisional Government were arrested and marched away.

October was a remarkably undramatic event. Nevsky Prospect filled with its usual crowds, the buses ran and theatres remained open, and the looting of the Palace's wine cellars was the only sign of the social levelling about to take place. Passive resistance to the coup came from the civil service who went on strike and armed resistance came from loyalist Cossacks who on 30 October failed to overcome a pro-Bolshevik force in an engagement at Pulkovo Heights outside of the capital. Fighting in Moscow lasted over a week before Bolshevik power was asserted, a foretaste of the Civil War that was soon to follow.

A reproduction of Vladimir Serov's famous painting 'Lenin proclaims soviet power'.

Revolution and Death

Who was to form a new government and how long could it last? A Congress of Soviets, scheduled for 25 October 1917, did not greet news of events with unanimous fervour. Just under half the delegates were Bolsheviks, and Right SRs and Mensheviks criticised the coup before walking out of the building and, as Trotsky memorably described their exit, 'into the dustbin of history'. It was left to the rest of the Congress to announce on 26 October a new, all-Bolshevik Council of People's Commissars, known as the Sovnarkom. This was the new government, with Lenin as its head and Trotsky in charge of foreign affairs. There was a general feeling that it could not last for long.

How democratic was the Bolshevik seizure of power? In November, elections for the Constituent Assembly went ahead as scheduled: Bolsheviks won only 25 per cent of the vote, the SRs nearly 40 per cent and the Kadet Party less than 10 per cent. These numbers were not as damaging to Lenin and his party as they seem. Bolshevism had not penetrated deep into the countryside, where the peasantry gave the SRs their vote, but where it did the rural vote was split between Bolsheviks and SRs, two parties with broadly similar land policies.

The SRs themselves were split, with Left SRs supporting the Bolsheviks, but this difference could not be reflected in the voting. Bolsheviks had a majority in most urban areas while support for them within the military was geographically split; the southern fronts and the Black Sea Fleet gave minority support, unlike the other armies and the Baltic Fleet which were solidly Bolshevik. Lenin did not accept the right of the Assembly to overrule Bolshevism. He argued that his party represented the interests of the majority and that counter-revolutionaries would only use the Assembly for their own ends. When the Assembly met on 5 January 1918, it was an anarchist supporter of the government who led an armed detachment and ordered the Assembly delegates to halt their debates and leave the building. The Assembly was dissolved by the government.

The problems and responsibilities facing the new government were on a colossal scale. There was a general breakdown of law and order, acts of summary justice became common, and the economy was in peril. It was impossible for one set of new rulers in Petrograd to control what was happening across the whole land. In urban areas, soviets of varying political complexions were wresting power from bourgeois interests while in the countryside and far-flung regions turmoil ruled. With the lid taken off centuries of tyranny and gross inequality, class hatred was unleashed and terrible atrocities were committed on all sides. At the same time, non-violent acts of social levelling spread across towns: housing committees forced the rich to share their generous living space with the disadvantaged; owners of safe-deposit boxes were forced to open them and hand over to the new state their contents of gold, diamonds and other valuables – including the occasional Fabergé egg. In south Russia and in the east of the Ukraine there was armed opposition to Bolshevik power and the cities there became magnets for those for whom the revolution spelt ruin. Fleeing princes and countesses rubbed shoulders with hard-headed businessmen, placing their hopes in a military overthrow of the barbarian Bolsheviks.

Lenin's priorities and those of the Bolshevik government as a whole were directed to settling the issues of the land and the war, distributing food to the cities and – the premise underlying all their efforts – retaining political power. Land was handed over to local soviets to divide up as they saw fit, a policy unashamedly adopted from the SR platform, with a largely ignored stipulation that the large estates of private landowners be maintained as single units.

Negotiations with the Germans had begun at the end of 1917 but Trotsky's stalling at the diplomatic table led to Russia's bluff being called when the Germans continued their advance in February 1918 and came within 400 miles of Petrograd. Lenin, knowing a German occupation of Russia would abort the revolution, saw the necessity of making a separate peace. He knew too that the October revolution was not the revolutionary spark that would set Europe blazing with revolt. Germany, he explained to the Central Committee, was only pregnant with revolution and the priority was to protect the healthy baby that had been born in October. It was a harsh summation and a defeat of cherished hopes. Lenin once again had to battle hard with opposing voices within the party, this time ones calling for a revolutionary war against Germany, but a humiliating treaty was finally signed on 3 March. The punitive terms of the Treaty of Brest-Litovsk meant the loss of the Ukraine, most of the Baltic and Poland. This amounted to half of Russia's industrial resources, over a third of its agriculture and nearly all its coalmines. For the Left SRs, who had joined Sovnarkom in December, this was a step too far and they left the government. In July, their erstwhile support turned into violent opposition when one of their leaders assassinated the German ambassador in an attempt to scupper the treaty.

In the first half of 1918 the threat of anti-Bolshevik armies, to be known as the White forces, was felt less keenly than the possibility that, even with the treaty signed, Petrograd would be occupied by the Germans. At this stage the fledgling Red Army was ill-equipped to defend Bolshevism. On 10 March the seat of government was transferred to Moscow and, once more, Lenin was on the move. In Petrograd the Smolny Institute had been his home and place of work, living with Krupskaya on the first floor and with his office close by on the second floor. When a break from the pressure of work became essential he could escape by simply leaving the build-ing and taking a stroll outside with Krupskaya. They could walk where they liked for few people knew what he looked like and the most powerful man in Russia passed unnoticed on the streets. The Kremlin was to be their home in Moscow but first they moved into the city's National Hotel and shared rooms with his sister Maria. The English writer Arthur Ransome described seeing Lenin sitting in the foyer of the hotel amidst his luggage, 'unimaginable rags and tatters of baggage and bedding rolled in blankets', and 'calm as usual, fearless as usual, without any guard whatsoever'.[91] This time his ano-nymity proved a hindrance and when he tried to enter the Kremlin his way was barred by a security guard who failed to recognise him.

By late March, Lenin, Krupskaya and Maria were installed in the Kremlin, in a four-roomed apartment on the third floor, and Lenin had easy access to the offices of various executive bodies. Lenin liked to walk around and chat to people from all corners of the country but this informality was balanced by his well-honed skills in organising and getting things done and his own office, also on the third floor, was characteristic in this respect. He sat on a plain wicker chair at his desk, using separate folders to prioritise his workload, and he had the bells on his telephones replaced by lights so as to minimise the level of interruption that calls occasioned. Unable to be separated for long from books, he had large bookcases installed. There was also room for some whimsy, including an old clock which never kept proper time and a figure on his desk of a monkey examining a human skull.

He was working too hard but he could not stop himself. There had been the promise of a brief respite in December 1917 when, along with Krupskaya and Maria, a short holiday had been taken in Finland but Lenin was unable to relax and spent the time there busily writing. The only ready break from work in Moscow came when he and Krupskaya enjoyed a walk by the side of the river, still inside the Kremlin but a place of peace and quiet. A country retreat was found for him in the village of Gorki, 20 miles south of the new capital, and for the remainder of his life, apart from a couple of visits back to Petrograd, Lenin spent his time either there or in Moscow. A lifetime of travelling and moving about was finally coming to an end; unfortunately, there would be little time left to enjoy.

The development of Russia after the events of October cannot be divorced from the corrosive impact of the Civil War. Russian society was polarised, if not traumatised, and the threat of foreign intervention designed to topple the government and restore capitalism permanently affected Bolshevik thinking – even after their military victory in 1920. The exigencies of the military situation and the sheer violence of armed conflict encouraged a defensive mentality that came to depend on brute force and centralised organisation. This, as much as anything else, did much to break the back of Lenin's hopes for post-revolutionary Russia. The level of support given to the Whites by Britain and other imperial powers was not decisive but it lengthened the course of the war and in this way contributed significantly to Russia's problems. The Civil War had a disastrous effect on an already-tottering economy and life in Petrograd ground to a halt as factories closed and over a million inhabitants fled. The fabric of ordinary life was torn asunder and when the Civil War did come to an end the country was in a state of chaos and close to utter collapse.

The demoralised armies of Russia had begun disintegrating in the course of the First World War as a result of desertions but it was the October Revolution that speeded up the process. The Civil War meant both sides had to rebuild their armed forces. The Red Army was formed under the direction of Trotsky, from Bolshevik soldiers and sailors at first but expanded by volunteers and the conscription of peasants. Thousands of ex-Tsarist officers were also conscripted, with their families often held as hostages. By the end of the Civil War, there were over five million men in the Red Army.

The demands of the Civil War vied with ideological considerations when it came to managing an economy near to collapse after 1917. Financial institutions were quickly brought under state control, something Lenin had always insisted on as an essential task of the revolution, and three quarters of industry was nationalised by late 1919. Free trade was ruthlessly curtailed by the need to requisition grain for the cities and armies, a practice also engaged in by the White Armies, and ideology contributed to a conflict between the peasantry and the government. Large-scale farming on collectivist principles appealed to the rulers in Moscow but this had little appeal to small farmers who wanted their own land to manage. The peasantry came up against the power of a new state which, arising out of the ashes of the Civil War, was increasingly dominated by the Bolshevik party. Sovnarkom, the Council of People's Commissars initially inaugurated as the nucleus of the new regime, lost ground to the Bolshevik Party's Central Committee. This may not have been something Lenin planned but it was allowed for given the fact that he was the formal head of the government and the *de facto* head of the Central Committee.

Could and should Lenin and the Bolsheviks have shared power with other parties? The SRs, with their roots in the countryside, the support of the peasantry and with a socialist programme, would seem to be natural and valuable allies. But they were not of one mind and the Right SRs became increasingly reactionary and intractable. Between February and October 1917 they acted as a conservative force and did not force the pace of agrarian reform; after October, they supported armed opposition to the government, and plotted first the kidnap and then the assassination of Lenin, inviting a repressive response from the Bolshevik government. The opposition of the Left SRs to a peace treaty with Germany became outright hostility to Sovnarkom and after the attempted assassination of the German ambassador their party was suppressed in July 1918. The Menshevik party also had its left and right wings and wavered in its attitude to the Bolsheviks from armed opposition to a lukewarm loyalism hedged with reservations. It remained a legal party until its suppression, begun at the end of 1920, accelerated after its support for the wave of strikes that broke out early in 1921.

Lenin was only prepared to share power with groups that fully supported Bolshevism – in effect, a way of not sharing power – because he did not trust any other party to maintain the iron discipline and ruthless will that he saw as absolutely essential in eliminating the threat posed by the bourgeoisie. Groups to the left, like the anarchists, were suppressed because their approach to socialism was regarded as a hindrance in the single-minded pursuit of this objective; as early as April 1918 the anarchists' Moscow headquarters was attacked by government forces.

The end of the First World War brought Lenin the hope of a revolution in Germany but by February 1919 Rosa Luxemburg had been murdered and an unsympathetic coalition government formed in the country with the support of the Social Democratic Party. Lenin's internationalism was not to be extinguished and in March the inaugural meeting of the Third International, to be known as the Comintern, took place in the Kremlin. Polish forces invaded western Ukraine at the height of the Civil War but were repulsed by the Red Army which reached the outskirts of Warsaw before being defeated in September 1920. While some historians see this as part of Lenin's aim to spread revolution to the West, others interpret it as a warning given to the West to keep out of Russian affairs.

Controversy about the Bolshevik dictatorship and the different ways in which it can be understood are deeply interwoven with questions about Lenin and his role after October 1917. Such areas of concern combine to form the basis for any final assessment of Lenin himself, the subject of the next chapter, but it is relevant to point out that Bolshevik thinking never pretended to be egalitarian or liberal when it came to dealing with political opposition. The Bolshevik Party identified itself as a party of the working class and its task, its reason for existence, was to break the class nature of Russian society. It did not think this could be accomplished without overcoming violent opposition from the bourgeoisie and rich peasants; the support of international capitalism for these class enemies was seen as confirmation of this. This encouraged, if it did not engender, an aggressive attitude towards dismantling the forces of reaction and creating in its wake a power structure based on the right of the working class to govern. Lenin, like many Bolsheviks, was ideologically prepared for a civil war even if he was unprepared for the scale and ferocity with which it would be conducted.

The Civil War was a multifaceted affair, fought over a vast area of land and involving an array of forces opposed, not always for the same reasons, to the Bolsheviks. As well as the White armies, there were nationalist and political groups who wanted to break away from Moscow and, in addition, a range of foreign forces – Britain, France, United States and Japan – opposing Bolshevism but motivated by their own complex of reasons. Added to this aggressive brew was the Czech Legion, originally intended to aid the Allies on the Western Front, which became a significant anti-Bolshevik force in Russia. White and Red armies struggled for control of Siberia, there was war in the south and White forces in Finland threatened Petrograd. The outcome of the war was decided in 1919. Admiral Kolchak advanced from the east as far as the Volga and other White armies under General Denikin, moving up from the south, came within 100 miles of Moscow. Early in 1920 the tide began to turn in favour of the Red Army, although General Wrangel's White forces remained a threat until he was forced into the Crimea in October 1920. The evacuation of his army the following month signalled the end of the Civil War, although large-scale peasant uprisings against Moscow rule continued and Japanese forces remained in parts of Siberia for another two years.

The intensification of the civil war hardened attitudes towards anyone regarded as anti-Bolshevik and the scale of non-judicial executions by the Cheka increased significantly. Lenin was not single-handedly masterminding the killing but he was unrepentant about it in principle, regarding such measures as necessary in the unfolding class war: *What do you want? Is it possible to act humanely in a struggle of such ferocity? Where is there any place for soft-heartedness or generosity? ... What is your criterion for judging which blows are necessary and which are superfluous in a fight?*[92] Lenin's acceptance of the need for executions and the use of terror was not something he agonised over. He had grown up in a world where such methods were often taken for granted and the clinical detachment that he could bring to matters of life and death was dispassionately applied to his own situation. This is shown by his behaviour in early July 1918 when he set off on a car journey with his chauffeur, Stepan Gil. On a visit to the former headquarters of the Left SRs, a group of armed Bolsheviks ordered the car Lenin was travelling in to stop and, before Gil could do so, shots were fired at them. No one was hurt and the over-zealous Bolsheviks were let off with a warning to be more careful in future.

The Cheka, a political police force introduced at the end of 1917, was not simply a sinister force manipulated by an evil Lenin. As 'The All-Russian Extraordinary Commission for Combating Counter-revolution and Sabotage' it had popular support and the slogan 'Death to the Bourgeoisie!', written on the walls of the Cheka interrogation rooms, was also a slogan to be found painted on walls around Moscow. The Civil War turned the Cheka into an organ of state terror, executing thousands without a trial for real or suspected anti-Bolshevik behaviour and generally mirroring the policies of Stolypin after the 1905 revolution.

On the same day, the car was stopped again by another group who, unconvinced as to the passenger's identity, took their country's leader to a police station under arrest.

Lenin laughed off such mishaps but the following month his relaxed attitude towards security almost cost him his life. He was returning to his car after delivering an open-air speech at a factory when he was shot by Fanny Kaplan, a member of a group of disaffected SRs. Stepan Gil drove him back to the Kremlin, thinking this was a safer destination than a public hospital, and the still-conscious Lenin made his way upstairs to his apartment and collapsed into a chair. *Is the end near? If it's near, tell me straight so that I don't leave matters pending.*[93] It was not until doctors arrived on the scene that the patient felt assured he would survive. What concerned Lenin in this most existential of moments was not his individual life but the history he was a player in and the need to deal with *matters pending*.

One of these was the fate of the former Imperial family. The Tsar and his family had been under arrest since his abdication but their privileged lifestyle continued in many respects, even when moved for their own safety to a town in Siberia. After October, everything changed. Trotsky planned a public trial of the Tsar but this was thwarted by the local Bolshevik soviet where the family was imprisoned. In July 1918 a decision was made to execute the Tsar and his family, out of fear that White forces might mount a rescue, and there is no reason to think Lenin had any moral or political objections to this course of action.[94]

As well as the military threat from the White armies, Lenin and his government also faced the challenging task of dealing with the problem of food distribution. The scale of the problem was enormous and more people died from hunger and disease in 1921–2 than from Russia's participation in the First World War and the Civil War combined. Those who lived, including the millions being demobilised from the Red Army, constituted a massive need as well as a source of discontent and Lenin became acutely aware of this. He was convinced that the problem lay with hoarding and profiteering by rich peasants and he had no hesitation in recommending drastic solutions. In August 1918, when the official in charge of collecting food in Saratov reported the need for army uniforms, equipment and ammunition in order to deal with the situation, Lenin immediately contacted the military authorities. In the meantime, he telegrammed back to the official, *I advise appointing your own chiefs and shooting conspirators and waverers without asking anybody and without allowing any idiotic red tape.*[95] Throughout the second half of 1918 Lenin was preoccupied with the Civil War and with the problem of getting food from the countryside into the cities. He was firing off telegrams daily, sometimes cajoling but more often demanding, and making it clear that rich peasants, kulaks, should answer with their lives if they hoarded grain in the hope of making profits. It should be said, too, that he also found the time to intervene on behalf of individuals when he thought they needed help: *I urgently request you to carry out a strict check and impartial examination of the matter, and allow Palinski passage to Poland*, he wrote in a telegram regarding the wrongful arrest of someone for counter-revolutionary activities.[96] The month before, July 1918, he telegraphed to a fellow Bolshevik: *Comrade Tsyurupa, You look ill. Without loss of time, take two months' holiday. If you do not promise this definitely, I shall complain to the Central Committee.*[97] Lenin's friendship with Gorky held firm, despite some fierce criticism from the writer, and he intervened more than once on behalf of individuals whom Gorky felt were being unfairly treated.

The demands made on Lenin and the demands he made on himself, practical and theoretical, during the years of the Civil War were enormous. The military situation was a source of constant pressure, as was the problem of distributing food, and there was a host of political considerations to be weighed in the balance. Trotsky and Stalin could agree on very little and Lenin worked hard to keep both of them focused on the common objective of securing military and political control of a highly uncertain situation. Paradoxically, the threat from White forces was a unifying factor in keeping sections of the population on the side of the Reds. White armies practised their own forms of terror, including the mass murder of Jews, expropriation of grain and their actions thwarted the separatist desires of minority groups like the Cossacks. White politics were repugnant to the majority of Russians and it was after their defeat that discontent began to focus itself on the Communist Party (as the Bolsheviks renamed themselves in March 1918).

The opposition to the Bolsheviks could not solely be attributed to counter-revolutionary forces and the waves of industrial unrest in 1920 included political demands from the left as well as general economic grievances. Similarly, the peasant revolt in the Ukraine, associated with the guerrilla leader Nestor Makhno, was inspired by an anarchist politics that was anti-Bolshevik but not anti-communist. The history of the changing relationship between anarchists and Bolsheviks goes to the heart of Lenin's tragic failures though just invoking a libertarianism versus authoritarianism antinomy is too simplistic. There were different groups of anarchists at work in revolutionary Russia: some wildly individualistic and utopian but others were well disposed to work with Bolsheviks in a common endeavour to create a new and better world. The Lenin of *The State and Revolution* hardly mentioned the role of the Party and a fundamental impetus behind the insurrectionary *Letters from Afar* was the conviction that people could demand the impossible, seize power and destroy the capitalist order. In October 1917, just weeks before the revolution, Lenin could speak in terms that many anarchists were willing to embrace: *When every labourer, every unemployed worker, every cook, every ruined peasant sees, not from newspapers, but with his own eyes, that the proletarian state is not cringing to wealth but is helping the poor, that this state does not hesitate to adopt revolutionary measures, that it confiscates surplus stocks of provisions from the parasites and distributes them to the hungry, that it forcibly installs the homeless in the houses of the rich ... .*[98] The possibility of anarchism influencing the development of the new Russia did not materialise. It was sacrificed in the exigencies of the Civil War and a firm belief that the fragility of the Bolshevik state, and its vulnerability as an affront to capitalism, required a firm centralism. For Lenin, the knot of power and the state needed grasping, not untying as anarchists wanted, and the call in *The State and Revolution* and *The April Theses* to smash the state withered on the vine.

Nestor Makhno, born in the Ukraine in 1889, led an anarchist force that united its black flag with a red one when he fought for the Bolsheviks against a White army invading the Ukraine. He visited Lenin in Moscow in 1918 but their alliance broke after the defeat of the White General Wrangel two years later, when the region sought to retain its anarchist autonomy. By the end of 1920, Makhno's army was smashed by the Red Army and the following year he went into exile and died in poverty and alcoholism in Paris.

Another theatre of conflict between anarchism and Bolshevism was in the naval base at Kronstadt, where anarchist ideas had some support, and where an uprising broke out in 1921. The Kronstadt sailors called for a return to the democracy of the soviets, freedom for other socialist parties and the disbandment of the Cheka. These demands were supported by many Bolshevik Party members at Kronstadt but Lenin and the Party leaders were not prepared to compromise. The order was given to take Kronstadt by force. The first armed assault by government forces on the naval base at Kronstadt failed but a second attack was mounted. Specially trained troops made their way across the ice and by 18 March the uprising was over. Executions and imprisonments followed. The radical credentials of the sailors of Kronstadt were not in doubt. They had been prepared for insurrection in July 1917 and in October came out solidly in support of the Bolsheviks. They rebelled against what they saw as a revolution being betrayed and the tragedy was that the Bolshevik government could only regard them as a threat to the success of the revolution. As with the revolutionary Irish government's decision to fire on its erstwhile supporters in the Four Courts in Dublin 1922, the order to attack Kronstadt was, if only symbolically, a fatal and self-inflicted blow to what the revolution stood for. The anarchists Emma Goldman and Alexander Berkman, deported from America in 1920, had returned to Russia in a spirit of hope for what the revolution there offered. When he heard the sound of gunfire directed at Kronstadt, Berkman wrote in his diary: 'Something has died within me'. At the end of 1921, when they left Russia in disillusionment, Berkman added: 'The revolution is dead; its spirit cried in the wilderness.'[99]

Events like the revolt of workers at Kronstadt and a major peasant uprising in Tambov forced Lenin to rethink the course of the revolution and the result in 1921 was the New

Economic Policy (NEP). The forced requisitioning of grain had failed and there was now a return to free trade in peasant surpluses and small-scale rural industries were encouraged. A system which gave a degree of independence to industry was also introduced. Lenin saw the reforms as an extension of what he called state capitalism, part of a programme he had outlined in 1918 when he called for increasing productivity, the introduction of competition, wage differentials and modern technology. *The possibility of building socialism depends exactly upon our success in combining the Soviet power and the Soviet organisation of administration with the up-to-date achievements of capitalism.*[100]

The organisation of administration concerned Lenin in the final years of his life as he became aware of a growing bureaucratism and careerism eating into the fruits of the revolution. The anarchist ideal celebrated in *The State and Revolution*, a self-governing, co-operatively organised society that would be truly democratic, had been seen as a natural antidote to an undemocratic centralism but this now seemed a far-off dream. Instead, the apparatus of the Bolshevik state was coming to resemble the Tsarist one and the opportunity this created for the emergence of a powerful manipulator was taking shape in the form of Stalin. In 1922 he became General Secretary of the Party, a position that gave him unrivalled control of the administrative organs of the state.

In grappling with the challenges of creating a socialist society, Lenin did not see the importance of creating a counter-culture along the lines that Bogdanov had earlier suggested. The building of a collectivist cultural alternative to the bourgeois mindset was a vision shared by a number of intellectuals and revolutionaries after October. They formed a group that became known as the Proletkult, from the Russian abbreviation of The Proletarian Cultural Educational Association. As a movement it developed a following of over 400,000 members, one in five of whom was engaged in running activities for workers in the years immediately after 1917. However, Bogdanov's influence on this non-party movement was sufficient to arouse Lenin's suspicions – at the end of 1920 he arranged publication of a second edition of the anti-Bogdanov *Materialism and Empiriocriticism* – and he ensured that Proletkult came under government control. Lenin did not welcome Proletkult's insistence on remaining outside the Party and neither could he sympathise with the avant-garde idea of an aesthetic break with the past as a correlative to a political rupture.

Lenin's well-documented preference for conservative art forms can be seen as emblematic of his attachment to political hegemony and his faith in the state as a vehicle for economic and political liberation. Far from being a philistine, though, Lenin believed that existing cultural forms, if available to everyone, provided the basis for enlightenment. Astonishingly, only a month after the October revolution, he was calling for the reorganising of Petrograd's public library:

(1) *The public library (the former Imperial Library) must immediately start an exchange of books with all public and state libraries in Petrograd and the provinces and with foreign libraries (in Finland, Sweden, etc.).*

(2) *The forwarding of books from one library to another must be made post-free by law.*

(3) *The library's reading-room must be open, as is the practice with private libraries and reading-rooms for the rich in civilized countries, from 8.00 a.m. to 11.00 p.m. daily, not excluding Sundays and holidays.*

(4) The required personnel must be immediately transferred to the Public Library from the various offices of the Ministry of Education (with more women, in view of the military demand for men), where nine-tenths of the staff are engaged not merely in useless, but in downright harmful work.[101]

Learning and literacy, not painting trees red or the art projects of the Constructivists, would liberate people and Lenin maintained a keen and detailed interest in educational reform between 1917 and 1922. He endorsed the idea of agit-trains travelling into the countryside and valued inexpensive reprints of literary classics more highly than experimental art forms. Lenin was equally conservative regarding family life and sexual mores and seems to have forgotten the spirit of Chernyshevsky's *What Is To Be Done?* when distancing himself from the efforts of people like Alexandra Kollontai and Inessa Armand to question traditional family relationships.

It was Lenin's tremendous will-power and total commitment that had driven his fellow Bolsheviks to replace the liberal revolution of February with a radical one in October. He relied on the same qualities to see him through the tumultuous years that followed. He was looking into a cauldron of civil war, economic turmoil, political differences and the almighty challenge of rebuilding a country on a new set of principles. To say the times were demanding would be an understatement and by relentlessly throwing his body and mind at the tasks facing him the outcome was perhaps inevitable. He was entering his fifties and 16-hour days began to take their toll; it took an attempted assassination to force a period of rest and even then he was back chairing Sovnarkom meetings within a couple of weeks.

Respite only came when he could retire to Gorky for a weekend and in July 1919 he enjoyed the company there of his sister Anna, whose husband Mark had died a few months earlier, and his brother Dmitri. Krupskaya was absent through her own work and her husband missed her: *The limes are in bloom. We had a good rest. I embrace you fondly and kiss you. Please rest more and work less.*[102] The death from cholera of Inessa Armand, whom he had last seen when she visited him in hospital after being shot, in September 1920 was a terrible blow. Lenin was by now admitting to feeling exhausted and a good night's sleep was becoming difficult; by the following year he was taking longer periods of rest but only between prolonged spells of intense work. Specialist doctors from within and outside of Russia were consulted but no agreed diagnosis had been reached when he suffered his first stroke in May 1922. Lenin slowly recovered with the help of Krupskaya and his sister Maria, and in October he returned to the Kremlin in spite of his doctors' protestations. It became obvious to everyone that Lenin, physically and mentally, was a broken man. Though increasingly suspicious of Stalin and convinced that his power needed curtailing, Lenin's health prevented him from acting and in December he suffered serious relapses. He knew now that his days were numbered and chose to spend what time he had left trying to preserve the gains of the revolution. He refused to return to Gorky and dictated his political testament, which included the following passage concerning Stalin: *Comrade Stalin, having become General Secretary, has concentrated unlimited power in his hands, and I am not convinced that he will always manage to use this power with sufficient care … . That is why I suggest that the comrades think about a way of removing Stalin from that post.*[103]

His assessment of Stalin was prescient but Lenin was too ill to act; by March 1923 there was very little he could do about anything, being paralysed on one side and unable to speak or sleep properly. In May he was carefully transported back to Gorky and looked after by Krupskaya and Maria. They turned down his repeated requests for poison, hoping against hope that his occasional good days presaged recovery. On one such occasion, in October, he insisted on being driven back to the Kremlin and was overcome by emotion when he stood in the room where as a member of Sovnarkom he had helped direct the course of the revolution and saved it from collapse. He survived until the new year, suffering another relapse and dying on the evening of 21 January of 1924. He was buried in Red Square on a fiercely cold afternoon, the crowd sung the *Internationale* and the trumpeters wiped vodka on their instruments to stop their breath freezing them to their lips.

The dedication of the Lenin Mausoleum in Red Square in 1930, on the 13th anniversary of the October Revolution.

Lenin's Legacy

Greatness is not generally attributed to Lenin: a point of view that has been common in the West for some time but one which is now also widespread in Russia and more so there than at any time since 1917. It seems that the most charitable attitude possible towards Lenin is one that allows for the sincerity of his aspirations while necessarily judging him guilty of a deep-seated authoritarianism, an innate fault that prepared the way for what happened under Stalin. The substantial charge against Lenin is that terror became a main weapon in his political arsenal and he used it to shore up a dictatorial regime. He stands for many as an example from history of what can go dreadfully wrong when democratic ideals are abandoned and, for many too, his now diminished importance stands for the welcomed death of Communism. It is now a familiar observation that to speak of the proletariat, never mind the dictatorship of that class, is part of an outmoded discourse; the whole Leninist vocabulary, like its mentality, belongs to a bygone time. Lenin's founding role in the creation of the Soviet state, while it continued to exist, gave him a supreme historical significance. The history of Europe between the two World Wars and the ideology of the

Cold War cannot be understood if October 1917 is taken out of the frame – constitutively speaking, it is the frame – and without Lenin there would have been no October. His importance was as indisputably real as the stone statues of him found throughout the Soviet empire. Now that the toppled statues, like the state he helped bring into existence, have been dismembered Lenin's proper place is seen by many to belong where Trotsky had earlier consigned the Mensheviks: in the dustbin of history. From this ideological perspective, Lenin's legacy is, belatedly and thankfully, a meagre one.

'Self-righteous, rude, demanding, ruthless, despotic, formalistic, bureaucratic, disciplined, cunning, intolerant, stubborn, one-sided, suspicious, distant, asocial, cold-blooded, ambitious, purposive, vindictive, spiteful, a grudgeholder, a coward who was able to face danger only when he deemed it unavoidable.'

Stefan T Possony[104]

'Saddam Hussein is now taking his rightful place alongside Hitler, Stalin, Lenin, Ceausescu in the pantheon of failed brutal dictators.'

Donald Rumsfeld, US Defense Secretary, 9 April 2003[105]

'At the very least, his extraordinary life and career prove the need for everyone to be vigilant. Not many historical personages have achieved this effect. Let thanks be given.'

Robert Service[106]

The broad charge against Lenin is that his pursuit of political objectives after October 1917 was dictatorial and terroristic, earning him a sizeable responsibility for the immense suffering of those years. Such accusations often ignore the impact of the Civil War in shaping the centralised bureaucratic machinery of what became the Soviet state. The war against the White armies helped create a Red Army numbering over five million by the end of the Civil War and the bureaucracy it spawned is often too glibly linked to the centralist ideas of Lenin. The actual number of troops fighting the White armies, amounting to about 10 per cent of the Red Army, required an enormous backup of personnel to handle the logistics involved in conducting a war over vast distances and on different fronts. An array of administrative structures was created by a government and country completely given over to the demands of war and as a consequence the soviets lost their power. In dealing a body blow to the soviets, militarisation destroyed the organs of working-class organisation that Lenin looked to for the implementation of his ideals. While only one in a hundred Bolsheviks in 1927 was like Lenin in having joined the party before 1917, over a third had joined in 1917–20 and were thus shaped by the Civil War.[107]

The soviets were also weakened by the growing power of the Cheka organisation, founded at the end of 1917 for the purpose of controlling outbreaks of looting in the turmoil of post-October Russia. The threat of anti-government forces subverting Bolshevism justified its widening powers and in the Civil War this led to summary executions. Civil wars usually give birth to atrocities on both sides and Russia was no exception to this. Bolsheviks were generally quite open about the use of terror in defeating 'class enemies' and there is Lenin's well-publicised directive to comrades in Penza of 11 August 1918 on how to deal with peasant resistance to the confiscation of grain.

1. Hang (hang without fail, so the people see) no fewer than one hundred known kulaks, rich men, bloodsuckers.

2. Publish their names.

3. Take from them all the grain.

4. Designate hostages – as per yesterday's telegram.

Do it in such a way that for hundreds of versts around, the people will see, tremble, know, shout: they are strangling and will strangle to death the bloodsucker kulaks.[108]

Many Bolsheviks took pride in their tough-mindedness and lack of illusion about the need for coercion and Lenin, supremely alert to the danger of a revolution being betrayed by a lack of will, saw the need for acts of exemplary brutality. *Capitalism cannot be defeated and eradicated without the ruthless suppression of the resistance of the exploiters.*[109] The Penza directive is regarded by critics as evidence of Lenin's innate moral depravity rather than an uncharacteristic display of murderous anger in the throes of a civil war and the possible defeat of the revolution.[110] Indisputably, he accepted the need for violence but he saw it as a necessary response to the violence that would be used by the old order. *Only mealy-mouthed petty-bourgeois and philistines can dream – deceiving thereby both themselves and the workers – of overthrowing capitalist oppression without a long and difficult process of suppressing the resistance of the exploiters ... the resistance will be fierce and desperate.*[111] Lenin lived in a world – and it is our world as well – where governments and ruling classes were willing to endorse obscene levels of violence and injustice in order to protect their interests. The nature of Tsarist rule and the course of the First World War had made this plain to Lenin and he made no bones about the need to use terror if it would protect the revolution. Out of two wrongs, a right would emerge. He wanted a different world, an end to the exploitation and injustice that he saw as endemic in the old one, and if this required ruthlessness and the willingness to use violence then so be it. Such a resolve would be temporary in nature and, playing a numbers game, he calculated success: *Since the 1905 revolution, Russia has been governed by 130,000 landowners, who have perpetrated endless violence against 150,000,000 people, heaped unconstrained abuse upon them, and condemned the vast majority to inhuman toil and semi-starvation. Yet we are told that the 240,000 members of the Bolshevik Party will not be able to govern Russia, govern her in the interests of the poor against the rich ... for the sake of high ideals and not for the sake of a fat sum received on the 20th of every month.*[112]

Lenin was equally unrepentant about the necessity for a dictatorship of the proletariat. *Never forget*, he wrote, the state *is simply a machine for the suppression of one class by another.* For Lenin, parliamentary democracy was an elaborate disguise, *because in fact it is freedom for the rich to buy and bribe the press, freedom for the rich to befuddle the people with venomous lies of the bourgeois press.* Democracy was *the dictatorship of the bourgeoisie, and for the emancipation of labour from the yoke of capital there is no other way but to replace this dictatorship with the dictatorship of the proletariat.*[113] Democracy for Lenin was not a mere matter of the franchise but about creating a state that did not exist to serve only the interests of the wealthy.

Lenin's putative lack of greatness is bound up with oft-repeated portrayals of him as someone with an extreme personality. He is judged as ruthlessly cruel, abnormally combative and intolerant, and pitilessly indifferent to human suffering. Such language is conveniently proffered as a mirror for the quality of his politics; so the more criticisms that can be made of the man the stronger the case for a condemnation of what he stood for. He is often portrayed as a philistine, obsessed with politics, driven by a repressed pathology or simply lacking the interiority that could have contributed to a more rounded personality. Aspects of his orderliness and punctiliousness – the fact that he sewed loose buttons back on to his jacket or kept his bicycle spotlessly clean – are listed as though faults of character. Facts like his rigorous work routines, conservative dress, preference for tidiness and keeping of careful records of expenditure are trotted out as suggestive of a manic individual; though just such qualities may well be aspects of the lifestyle of most of those writers who, content with their own sense of individuality, cannot resist chipping away at Lenin's core. He is supposed to have confessed, after listening to a performance of Beethoven's Appassionata, that it made him feel sentimental and want to pat the heads of people when he knew really that the task was to beat them on the head without mercy. This anecdote is often referred to as characteristic of a man with a hard heart, unwilling to trust his emotions but too willing to inflict violence on others.[114]

Apart from two years spent as a lawyer Lenin never had a proper job and, so it goes, he supported himself with an income that came from his mother's estate. The first observation is immaterial – as well as sitting uneasily with his reputation as a workaholic – and any truth to the second one requires a more nuanced understanding of his finances. Lenin's mother was not rich but as a widow she managed her resources very sensibly and helped her children whenever she could. Lenin depended on pay from the party and sometimes experienced periods of hardship, as in Switzerland during the First World War. Lenin's alleged heartlessness is also at odds with some of the facts. When Krupskaya was suffering from her thyroid condition in 1913, Lenin sought out an expensive specialist for her even though this put a considerable strain on their meagre funds. Towards those he felt close to, there was a deep commitment and strength of feeling on Lenin's part that he never felt the need to make public or dramatise. Between April and October 1917, his time was as lacking in routine as anyone could possibly imagine. It was an intensely exciting and dangerous period and there was an existential edge to his life then that most of those who have written about and pronounced judgement on his personality have never experienced. In those heady days after his arrival back in Russia, he was 47 years of age, owned nothing and had nowhere he could call a home. Possessions, material or monetary, meant nothing to him or Krupskaya and a more bohemian kind of existence is not easy to envisage. During those tumultuous months he lived on the hoof, more separated from Krupskaya than at any time since the end of his exile in Siberia, and yet their loyalty and love for one another remained constant.

A more humane and rounded individual than the one most often portrayed emerges from the memoirs of those who knew Lenin. Nikolai Valentinov, who got to know him in Geneva in 1904 but later came to reject his politics, remembered a benevolent Lenin who went out of his way to help him when in difficulty.[115] Valentinov's portrayal is of a man keenly interested in sports and keeping fit, someone who liked singing and who vigorously defended the classics of Russian literature against the charge that because they were written by members of a landowning nobility their worth was necessarily diminished.

Lenin's personality was complex and the artist Claire Sheridan sensed this when she observed: 'Never did I see anyone make so many faces. Lenin laughed and frowned, and looked thoughtful, sad, and humorous all in turn.'[116] Such a person cannot be easily reduced to adjectives and anecdotes indicating obsession, anger, narrow-mindedness and so on; and it is not explainable by a simplistic psychology in terms of being a spoilt child or a repressed psyche driven to inhuman extremes. Lenin himself would dismiss any discussion of his personality as irrelevant and, as someone who stood by his politics alone, in an important sense he was right. He was a private person and although he cared deeply for his family he was not particularly exercised by other people's personal opinions – and this extended to their personal opinions of him. Other people's politics mattered and his political relationships with them mattered but as regards the rest he was largely indifferent, and he thought this should be the proper attitude on the part of others towards his own personality and private life. When asked why, from among the many pseudonyms used, he stuck with the Lenin one he mockingly replied: *You'll grow old if you know too much*.[117] His complete unpretentiousness could be seen as a lack of pride and it was a characteristic which disconcerted Stalin: 'I had hoped to see the mountain eagle of our party, the great man, great physically as well as politically. I had fancied Lenin as a giant, stately and imposing. How great was my disappointment to see a most ordinary-looking man, below average height, in no way, literally in no way, distinguishable from ordinary mortals ... . Usually a great man comes late to a meeting so that his appearance may be awaited with bated breath ... [Lenin] arrived at the conference before the other delegates were there and had settled himself somewhere in a corner and was unassumingly carrying on a conversation, with the most ordinary delegates. I will not conceal from you that at that time this seemed to be to be rather a violation of certain essential rules.'[118]

There are aspects to Lenin that remain hidden because he chose not to address them in writing and of these the most interesting is his ethical dimension, that part of his self that was bound up with a set of core values and commitments. Such a way of viewing Lenin contradicts the more familiar take on him as someone whose excessive libidinal investment in politics rendered his personal relationships both ethically and emotionally bankrupt. The Lenin of such clichés is not the person who, arriving in Petrograd on the morning of 4 April 1917, put the revolution on hold and journeyed to the cemetery where his mother and sister were buried. The point being made goes further than this – for the sense of a moral code that must be acted *on* and *from*, not merely in accordance *with*, informs his politics at the deepest possible level. This ethical subjectivity goes back to his childhood and early years, nurtured by his parents and the examples they set, strengthened by the nature and fate of his older brother and resonating in his experience of reading and re-reading Chernyshevsky's *What Is To Be Done?*. It was simply wrong for a minority of rich people to enjoy a selfish and privileged existence at the expense of the majority of people – this was the moral force guiding the pronouncements of *The State and Revolution* and *Letters from Afar* – and Lenin devoted his life to changing this state of affairs. He did not fully understand the philosophical bombshell that Marx exploded in *Theses on Feuerbach* but he took to heart the final thesis about not interpreting the world but changing it. This was his ethical choice – revolution, not resignation – and the enduring value of Lenin's legacy is that he acted on his ethics and took the risks that this entailed.

This view of Lenin, as someone truly great and possessing an ongoing momentous importance, is not generally prevalent and it is only in writers like Alain Badiou and Slavoj Žižek that one can find such an endorsement of his enduring significance. For Badiou, Lenin's emancipatory politics are exemplary in their expression of 'the passion for the real' that so singularly defined the century between 1917 and the end of the 1970s.[119] Lenin recognised a moment that went

Alain Badiou is one of the most politically engaged and radical of
contemporary French philosophers. His most important work is *Being
and Event* (1988) although *The Century* (2005) is a more accessible
introduction to his thought. For Badiou, an Event signals the
unpredictable and contingent way in which the political and
epistemological bedrock of an existing order is shaken from within by a
dimension that until then has not been acknowledged. This very
different dimension has always been there but is only recognised as
such from the standpoint of the Event and in this way it emerges as an
Event of Truth that traverses the existing order of knowledge. An
Event, like October 1917 or the French Revolution, cannot be predicted
because it emerges from forces that are not admitted by the *status
quo*.

Slavoj Žižek, a Slovenian born in 1949, is a philosopher and
psychoanalyst whose prodigious and stimulating output of books and
articles has made him the most exciting and provocative cultural
theorist of current times. Fiercely opposed to postmodernism and
liberal politics, Žižek's heady blend of Hegel, Marx and Lacan has
earned him detractors as well as admirers. Along with Badiou, he writes
in a novel way that avoids the usual characterisation of Lenin as a
power-hungry ideologue who prepared the way for Stalin and
totalitarianism.

beyond the failed promises of previous revolutions, beyond
the collapse of the Paris Commune, and he was not afraid to
accept the challenge that this moment presented. There was
the chance of a revolution overturning those who sought to
benefit from the first revolution of February and the chance
lay in the gap that had been opened up by the overthrow of
Tsarism. The first revolution created the possibility for a new
form of politics to emerge and it required imagination, discipline and commitment to envisage this.

Situating Lenin's greatness in these terms, Žižek cham-
pions the need to repeat the Lenin who was thrown into a
unique situation in 1917, one where old orthodoxies had gone
up in smoke when European socialist parties had supported

the First World War. The catastrophe of 1914 signalled the collapse of progressive politics but Lenin bit that bullet and reinvented a revolutionary project, insisting in the face of 'facts' the possibility of a proletarian revolution that would provide the form for a new way of organising life and politics. The dictatorship of the proletariat was a form that sought to confront the inherent dictatorship of power that underlay liberal democracy and institute instead a radical emancipatory politics.[120] For Žižek, the philosophical significance of Lenin resides in his affirmation 'that universal truth and partisanship, the gesture of taking sides, are not only mutually exclusive, but condition each other: the *universal* truth of a concrete situation can be articulated only from a thoroughly *partisan* position; truth is, by definition, one-sided.'[121] To repeat Lenin is not to return to what he did and repeat the failure but to resurrect the utopian, subversive flame that burned within him and repeat his resolve to think anew in the face of a present catastrophe. Žižek writes: 'This is the gap between revolution in the sense of the imaginary explosion of universal solidarity when "everything seems possible" and the hard work of social reconstruction which must be performed if this explosion is to leave any traces in the social edifice. This gap – which recalls the interval between 1789 and 1793 in the French revolution – is the space of Lenin's unique intervention. The fundamental lesson of revolutionary materialism is that revolution must strike twice. It is not that the first moment has the form of revolution, with the substance having to be filled in later, but rather the opposite: the first revolution retains the old mindset, the belief that freedom and justice can be achieved if we simply use the already-existing state apparatus and its democratic mechanisms, that the "good" party might win a free election and implement the socialist transformation "legally" … Those who oscillate, and are afraid to take the second step of overcoming the old forms, are those who (in Robespierre's words) want a "revolution without revolution".'[122]

The strength of Lenin's determination to challenge capitalism and the self-belief that propelled him to risk driving his party beyond February 1917 are inseparable from his willingness to use violence and terror if such tactics were used against the Bolsheviks. He fully expected this to be the case, as indeed it was, and he had no hesitation in replying in kind. History had shown Lenin how the interests of capitalists could emerge on top from revolutionary uprisings of the dispossessed – he knew that the Paris Commune was crushed after 72 days by the military forces of the future first president of the Third Republic and 20,000 Parisians slaughtered – and he had no intention of allowing this to be repeated after October. He was prepared to tackle opposition head-on with no holds barred, and sometimes this was taken to excess, but to take this away would be to remove the dynamism and willpower that turned February into October. The idealistic hopes expressed in *The State and Revolution*, and they were ethical as much as political ideals, collapsed in the violent throes of a civil war. They died, too, because they were based on an uneasy and unquestioned partnership of state and people power.

Lenin knew that politics could access the constitutive consciousness that would effect radical change and he refused to accept that the way things are is the way they should be allowed to be. In 'The Immediate Tasks of the Soviet Government', published in April 1918, he stressed the need for 'iron discipline' and unquestioning obedience to authority in the workplace as the corollary to the Bolshevik monopoly over political power. He extolled fellow Bolsheviks to behave and work by the principles that always informed his own approach to life: *Keep regular and honest accounts of money, manage economically, do not be lazy ... people with sober and practical minds will be promoted.*[123] This was what had worked for him as a student in Simbirsk and got him his external law degree in half the time it took others. It was what had launched *Iskra* and kept him going in the years of exile across the cities of Europe. He knew the importance of discipline, ultimately it helped account for the success of the West, and if the power of the bourgeoisie was to be broken for good then the proletariat had to acquire it with the same depth and force. He took it as given that the required organisational discipline, embodied in the state, had to be of the same kind as what had gone before. In *The State and Revolution*, there is an antinomy between the urge to destroy the state and the need to retain its functionality as a means of change. Lenin did not confront the inherent difficulties produced by such an antinomy and Russia ended up with the wrong kind of state. The antinomy was not acknowledged, let alone confronted, and thus could not be resolved.

How one finally judges Lenin is as much, if not more, a reflection of one's own political philosophy as it is of the man himself. A chance to change the world came after February 1917 when it was possible to think the impossible and Lenin's greatness was to seize the chance and ensure that the bourgeoisie did not reap the benefits of an anti-autocratic revolution. To realistically bring this about, given the onset of a civil war, required a willingness to use violent and ruthless measures. Lenin did not pretend otherwise or make excuses for the brutality it entailed. This determined resolve to destroy capitalism led him from the library in Zurich in April 1917 to a bus stop in Petrograd on the evening of 24 October. It also accounts for Lenin's continuing resistance to academia's recycling of radical thinkers into non-threatening figures fit for cultural digestion; hence his unpopularity, if not invisibility, in contemporary political and social thought. Lenin was not a tragic hero – he was certainly no Hamlet – but, bearing in mind how the source of the downfall of the classic tragic hero is inseparable from the quality that constitutes his greatness, there is something tragic as well as heroic about his life's endeavour, his existential fidelity to the Event of October 1917 and his willingness to risk all for the sake of a more just world.

Notes

1. The old-style Julian calendar, which was maintained in Russia until January 1918, makes its dates 12 days behind the modern Gregorian calendar in the 19th century and 13 days behind in the 20th century. The dates in this book follow the Russian calendar that was in use at the time. Berlin was planned to be taken on 22 April 1945.

2. A population census in 1897 recorded the military as making up 17 per cent of the population: Dmitri Volkognov, *Lenin: Life and Legacy* (HarperCollins, London: 1994) p 3.

3. Her name was Anna Ivanovna Grosschopf and her father's family came from Lübeck while her mother, Anna Estedt, had a Swedish background.

4. The Russian biographer, though, who claims 'Lenin's somewhat Asiatic appearance' is attributable to the Kalmyk ingredient (Volkognov, *Lenin: Life and Legacy*, p 7) is not alone in linking aspects of Lenin's physical appearance to supposed ethnic factors.

5. Edmund Wilson, *To the Finland Station* (Fontana, London: 1974) p 358.

6. Wilson, *To the Finland Station*, p 358.

7. N Valentinov, *Encounters with Lenin* (Oxford University Press, Oxford: 1968) p 107.

8. As with many aspects of Lenin's life, details of his schooling owe much to the scholarship of Robert Service and his biography *Lenin* (Pan Books, London: 2002).

9. Christopher Read, *Lenin* (Routledge, London: 2005) p 9.

10. N Valentinov, *The Early Years of Lenin* (University of Michigan, Ann Arbor: 1969) p 26.

11. Trotsky provides a detailed account of the circumstances surrounding their arrest in *The Young Lenin* (David and Charles, Newton Abbot: 1972) pp 57–69.

12. Lenin's wife recalls him telling her how the family were shunned and how no-one was willing to accompany Maria Alexandrovna on her journey to the capital: 'All acquaintances shunned the Ulyanov family. Even an aged teacher, who had formerly come every evening to play chess, left off calling … Vladimir Ilyich told me that this widespread cowardice made a very profound impression upon him at that time.' Nadezhda Krupskaya, *Memories of Lenin* (Panther, London: 1970) p 17.

13. Service, *Lenin*, p 60.

14. David Shub, *Lenin* (Penguin, London: 1966) p 31.

15. Volkogonov, *Lenin: Life and Legacy*, p 16. Volkogonov is quoting from an account by Alexander's lawyer who was present at the last meeting in the prison between Maria and her son.

16. The sentence of death was commuted to deportation at the last moment; the Tsar withholding a pardon until Dostoyevsky and fellow 'conspirators' were standing on the scaffold.

17. Nikolai Chernyshevsky, *What Is To Be Done?*, translated by Michael R Katz (Cornell University Press, Ithaca: 1989) p 313.

18. Robert Service, *Lenin: A Political Life*, Vol. 1 (Macmillan, London: 1985) p 32. The powerful influence of Chernyshevsky is also recorded in Valentinov, *Encounters with Lenin*, pp 66–8.

19. Valentinov, born nine years after Lenin, was in no doubt about why Marxism seized the minds of people like himself in Russia: 'Marxism came from Europe. It did not smell and taste of home-grown mould and provincialism, but was new, fresh, and exciting. Marxism held out a promise that we would not stay a semi-Asiatic country, but would become part of the West with its culture, institutions and attributes of a free political system. The West was our guiding light.' Valentinov, *Encounters with Lenin*, p 23.

20. Lenin, *Collected Works* (Progress Publishers, Moscow: 1977) Vol. 37, pp 465–6, hereafter *Collected Works*. This edition of the *Collected Works* is accessible at *www.Marxists.org* and quotations in this book, unless otherwise indicated, are taken from the website. Some of the texts on the website are taken from an earlier, 1972 edition of the collected works by Progress Publishers.

21. *Collected Works*, Vol. 37, pp 65–6.

22. *Collected Works*, Vol. 37, pp 67–8.

23. Some accounts suggest Krupskaya was not attractive, and she did later develop a thyroid condition that affected her appearance, but photographs of her around this time suggest the opposite and this is also the opinion of her biographer Robert H McNeal in *Bride of the Revolution* (Victor Gollancz, London: 1973) p 51.

24. 'I try to maintain something of a diet – and you brought such enormous quantities that I think it will last me almost a week and get as hard as the Sunday pie at Oblomovka.' *Collected Works*, Vol. 37, pp 85–6. In Goncharov's comic novel *Oblomov*, a baked pie is so enormous that a family eats it for two days, the servants cannot finish it over another two days and one brave soul takes to finishing the hardened remains.

25. A letter to his mother in August 1897, in *Collected Works*, Vol. 37, pp 123–5.

26. Krupskaya remembers him saying, '"If we meet any hares, I won't fire as I didn't bring any straps, and it won't be convenient to carry them." Yet immediately a hare darted out Vladimir Ilyich fired.' Krupskaya, *Memories of Lenin*, p 37.

27. *Collected Works*, Vol. 37, pp 150–4.

28. 'How the "Spark" Was Nearly Extinguished', *Collected Works*, Vol. 4, pp 331–49.

29. *What Is To Be Done?* in Lenin, *Essential Works of Lenin*, ed. Henry M Christman (Dover Publications, New York: 1987), p 67 (*Collected Works*, Vol. 5, pp 347–530), hereafter *What Is To Be Done?*.

30. *What Is To Be Done?*, p 85.

31. *What Is To Be Done?*, p 105.

32. Marcel Liebman, *Leninism Under Lenin* (Merlin Press, London: 1975) p 26.

33. *What Is To Be Done?*, p 150.

34. *Collected Works*, Vol. 5, *What Is To Be Done? Can A Newspaper Be A Collective Organiser?* (This section is not included in *Essential Works of Lenin*.)

35. Lenin wasted little time in applying for a reader's ticket to the British Museum's Reading Room. Using another

pseudonym, Jacob Richter, his ticket was initially issued for three months, later extended for another three months and then six months. Lenin, punctilious as always, handed back his ticket before leaving London a year later.

36. The Holford Square address tended to be only used for trusted correspondents and other addresses were commonly employed for *Iskra* matters. These included Alexeev's flat in Frederick Street and a flat at 20 Regent Square, home to a Marxist couple that Lenin and Krupskaya had known in St Petersburg. Another address that was used for a while was 26 Granville Square and, when Alexeev moved there in the autumn of 1902, so too was 22 Ampton Street. All these addresses were conveniently reached from Holford Square. Other addresses used included 85 Avenell Road, 62 Mildmay Grove and 26 Barsett Road.

37. L Muravyova and I Sivolap-Kaftanova, *Lenin in London* (Progress Publishers, Moscow: 1983) pp 77–8. Gorky, who met Zalomov and may have edited the speech, based his *Mother* on the demonstration by factory workers near Nizhni Novgorod which led to Zalomov's arrest and trial.

38. Valentinov, *Encounters with Lenin*, p 43. Chernyshevsky, *What Is To Be Done?*, p 316.

39. Krupskaya, *Memories of Lenin*, p 75.

40. Krupskaya, *Memories of Lenin*, p 76.

41. The Bund, the General Union of Lithuanian, Polish and Russian Jewish Workers, were granted a disproportionately small number of delegates to the Congress and, angry at having their proposal for regional autonomy turned down by the Congress, walked out in protest. Had they remained, they would have supported

Martov and prevented his group being designated a minority.

42. *Collected Works*, Vol. 37, p 363.

43. Ewa M Thompson, 'Russophilia', in *Chronicles* (Oct. 1994) pp 32–5, quoted in Norman Davies, *Europe* (Oxford University Press: 1996) p 869.

44. Richard Pipes, *The Russian Revolution* (HarperCollins, London: 1992) p 14.

45. Quoted by Lenin in 'The Beginning of the Revolution in Russia', written three days after Bloody Sunday, *Collected Works*, Vol. 8, pp 97–100.

46. Lenin, 'New Tasks and New Forces', published 23 February 1905, *Collected Works*, Vol. 8, pp 209–20.

47. Orlando Figes, *A People's Tragedy* (Pimlico, London: 1996) p 202.

48. The church, at the corner of Balmes Road and Southgate Road, is no longer standing.

49. Krupskaya, *Memories of Lenin*, p 146.

50. Lenin, 'Social-Democracy and the Provisional Revolutionary Government', *Collected Works*, Vol. 8, pp 275–92.

51. Lenin, 'The Slogans and Organisation of Social-Democratic Work Inside and Outside the Duma', published in 1911, *Collected Works*, Vol. 17, pp 331–41.

52. Berkeley had in mind the philosophy of John Locke, whose *Essay Concerning Human Understanding* was published in 1690. Berkeley's *A Treatise Concerning the Principles of Human Knowledge* appeared 20 years later and this is the book Lenin is referring to.

53. 'The chief defect of all hitherto existing materialism – that of Feuerbach included – is that the thing, reality, sensuousness, is conceived only in the form of the *object*

or of *contemplation* but not as *human sensuous activity, practice*, not subjectively.' Marx, 'Theses on Feuerbach', in *Marx and Engels: Basic Writings on Politics and Philosophy*, ed. Lewis S Feuer (Fontana, London: 1974) p 283.

54. A letter to Anna, 8 April 1909. *Collected Works*, Vol. 37, pp 426–7.

55. Valentinov, *Encounters with Lenin*, p 141.

56. Maxim Gorky, *Days With Lenin*, quoted in Ronald W Clark, *Lenin* (Faber and Faber, London: 1989) p 135.

57. Michael Pearson, *Lenin's Mistress* (Random House, New York: 2001).

58. Letter to Gorky, 11 April 1910. *Collected Works*, Vol. 34, pp 419–22.

59. Letter to his mother, 1 July 1912. *Collected Works*, Vol. 37, pp 479–80.

60. Pearson, *Lenin's Mistress*, p 107.

61. Lenin was convinced that the report of this in the daily newspaper of the German Social Democrats was a forgery.

62. Alexander Solzhenitsyn, *Lenin in Zurich* (Penguin, London: 1977); Tom Stoppard, *Travesties* (Faber and Faber, London: 1975).

63. Krupskaya, *Memories of Lenin*, p 271.

64. *Collected Works*, Vol. 38, p 359.

65. The importance of Lenin's reading of Hegel is discussed in detail in Part II of *Lenin Reloaded: Towards a Politics of Truth*, eds. Budgen, Kouvelakis and Žižek (Duke University Press, Durham and London: 2007).

66. Krupskaya, *Memories of Lenin*, p 252.

67. Letter, 16 January 1916, *Collected Works*, Vol. 43, pp 505–6.

68. Lenin, *Imperialism: The Highest Stage of Capitalism* in *Essential Works of Lenin*, ed. Christman, p 216 (*Collected Works*, Vol. 22), hereafter *Imperialism*.

69. *Imperialism*, p 231.

70. *Imperialism*, p 236.

71. Most notably, the work of the British liberal economist J A Hobson and the Austrian Marxist Rudolf Hilferding.

72. *Imperialism*, p 269.

73. 'I hardly spoke to Ilyich that night – there were really no words to express the experience, everything was understood without words.' Krupskaya, *Memories of Lenin*, p 296.

74. Slavoj Žižek (ed.), *Revolution At The Gates* (Verso, London: 2002) p 21; *Collected Works*, Vol. 23.

75. Lenin, 'The Tasks of the Proletariat in the Present Revolution', in Žižek (ed.), *Revolution At The Gates*, p 56; *Collected Works*, Vol. 24, pp 21–9.

76. Clark, *Lenin*, p 219.

77. Krupskaya, *Memories of Lenin*, p 301.

78. Quoted in Sheila Fitzpatrick, 'The Rise and Fall of the Baggy-Trousered Barbarians', *London Review of Books* (19 Aug 2004).

79. The Provisional Government had restricted the sale of wigs for just the kind of reason that Lenin used one but, with the excuse that a railwaymen's amateur theatre group required one for their show, a Bolshevik colleague obtained one.

80. Pipes, *The Russian Revolution*, p 434.

81. Lenin, 'The Impending Catastrophe and How To Combat It', in Žižek (ed.), *Revolution At The Gates*, p 78 (*Collected Works*, Vol. 25, pp 323–69).

82. Lenin, 'One of the Fundamental Questions of the Revolution', in Žižek (ed.), *Revolution At The Gates*, p 108 (*Collected Works*, Vol. 25, pp 370–7).

83. Lenin, 'One of the Fundamental Questions of the Revolution', in Žižek (ed.), *Revolution At The Gates*, p 112 (*Collected Works*, Vol. 25, pp 370–7).

84. Christopher Hill, *Lenin* (The English University Press, London: 1961) p 104.

85. Lenin, 'Letters from Afar', in Žižek (ed.), *Revolution At The Gates*, p 44 (*Collected Works*, Vol. 23, pp 295–342).

86. Lenin, *The State and Revolution* in *Collected Works*, Vol. 25, pp 381–492; quotations that follow in this chapter, unless otherwise stated, are from *The State and Revolution*.

87. *Collected Works*, Vol. 43, p 638.

88. Lenin, 'The Crisis Has Matured', in Žižek (ed.), *Revolution At The Gates*, p 141 (*Collected Works*, Vol. 26, pp 74–85).

89. Lenin, 'Letter to Comrades', in Žižek (ed.), *Revolution At The Gates*, pp 145–6 (*Collected Works*, Vol. 26, pp 195–215).

90. *Collected Works*, Vol. 43, p 638.

91. Hugh Brogan, *The Life of Arthur Ransome* (Jonathan Cape, London: 1984) p 187.

92. According to Gorky, this is how Lenin replied to the criticisms of the writer. Quoted in Clark, *Lenin*, pp 382–3.

93. Quoted in Service, *Lenin*, p 369.

94. It seems likely that the Bolshevik government in Moscow was aware of plans for the execution; descendants of the Romanov dynasty claim that Lenin was actively involved

in giving the order. See *The Independent on Sunday* (16 Apr 2006).

95. *Collected Works*, Vol. 44, pp 139–40.

96. *Collected Works*, Vol. 44, p 118.

97. *Collected Works*, Vol. 44, p 121.

98. *Collected Works*, Vol. 26, pp 87–136.

99. Alexander Berkman, *The Bolshevik Myth: Diary 1920–1922* (Hutchinson, London: 1925) pp 303 and 319.

100. Lenin, 'The Immediate Tasks of the Soviet Government', April 1918, *Collected Works*, Vol. 27, pp 235–77.

101. *Collected Works*, Vol. 28, p 351.

102. 15 Jul 1919, *Collected Works*, Vol. 37, p 546.

103. Lenin, '[Last] Testament', *Collected Works*, Vol. 36, pp 593–611.

104. Stefan T Possony, *Lenin: The Compulsive Revolutionary* (Henry Regnery Co., Chicago: 1964), quoted in Paul LeBlanc, *Marx, Lenin, and the Revolutionary Experience* (Routledge, New York: 2006) p 78.

105. *www.defenselink.mil/news/apr2003* (accessed 25 Aug 2008).

106. The concluding sentences of Service, *Lenin*, p 494.

107. Sheila Fitzpatrick, *The Russian Revolution* (Oxford University Press: 1984) p 64.

108. Richard Pipes, *The Unknown Lenin* (Yale University Press, New Haven: 1998) p 50. The directive was first brought to light in a Russian newspaper in 1992.

109. Lenin, 'The Immediate Tasks of the Soviet Government', April 1918, *Collected Works*, Vol. 27, pp 235–77.

110. An extreme example of this is Richard Pipes but Robert Service is also severe in his judgement: 'He reverted the practices of twentieth-century European war to the Middle Ages. No moral threshold was sacred' (*Lenin*,

p 366). Christopher Read offers a more balanced account: 'It was absolutely crucial to Lenin's strategy that the majority would hold very firm against the recalcitrant minority in the early days and quickly break the remnants of its power. It explains the uncharacteristic ferocity and, occasionally, near-hysterical bloodthirstiness, apparent in a few of his statements of the early months': Read, *Lenin*, pp 201–2.

111. Lenin, 'Democracy and Dictatorship', written in 1918. *Collected Works*, Vol. 28, pp 368–72.

112. Lenin, 'Can the Bolsheviks Retain State Power?', October 1917. *Collected Works*, Vol. 26, pp 87–136.

113. Lenin, 'Democracy and Dictatorship'.

114. For example, Figes, *A People's Tragedy*, p 390 and Service, *Lenin*, p 273.

115. Valentinov, *Encounters with Lenin*, pp 86–93.

116. Quoted in LeBlanc, *Marx, Lenin, and the Revolutionary Experience*, p 83.

117. Valentinov, *Encounters with Lenin*, p 45.

118. Quoted in Isaac Deutscher, *Stalin: A Political Biography* (Oxford University Press: 1949) p 78.

119. Alain Badiou, *The Century* (Polity Press, Cambridge: 2007) p 32.

120. See Žižek's introduction to *Virtue and Terror: Maximilien Robespierre* (Verso, London: 2007) pp xxvi-vii.

121. Žižek (ed.), *Revolution At The Gates*, p 177.

122. Slavoj Žižek, 'Revolution Must Strike Twice', *New Left Review* (25 Jul 2002) p 13.

123. Lenin, 'The Immediate Tasks of the Soviet Government', written in 1918. *Collected Works*, Vol. 27, pp 235–77.

Chronology

YEAR	AGE	LIFE
1870		10 Apr: Vladimir Ilyich Ulyanov (Lenin) born in Simbirsk, Russia.
1886	15	Lenin's father dies at the age of 53.
1887	17	Alexander Ulyanov, Lenin's older brother, is executed for his part in an attempted assassination of the Tsar. Four months after entering Kazan University, Lenin is arrested in a student demonstration.
1889	19	Moves with his family to Samara and joins clandestine group of intellectuals.
1891	21	Passes law examination as an external student at St Petersburg University.
1894	23	Living in St Petersburg, attends a Marxist meeting and meets Nadezhda Krupskaya.
1895	25	Travels abroad between May and September and meets Plekhanov. In December, arrested in St Petersburg.
1897	26	Sentenced to three years of exile in Siberia.

YEAR	HISTORY	CULTURE
1870	Napoleon III declares war against Prussia. Paris besieged.	Charles Dickens dies.
1886	Irish Home Rule Bill introduced by Prime Minister Gladstone.	Thomas Hardy, *The Mayor of Casterbridge*.
1887	Police clash with pro-Irish independence protesters in what becomes known as 'Bloody Sunday'.	Birth of Marc Chagall and Marcel Duchamp.
1889	Second Socialist International set up in Paris. Great London Dock Strike.	The first issue of the *Wall Street Journal* is published.
1891	Troops fire on and kill workers at a May Day demonstration in support of eight-hour workday in Fourmies, France. Building of the Trans-Siberian Railroad begins.	George Gissing, *New Grub Street*.
1894	Tsar Alexander III dies and is succeeded by his son Nicholas II. The Dreyfus affair begins in France.	Anthony Hope, *The Prisoner of Zenda*.
1895	Cuba rebels against Spanish rule.	Chekhov, *The Seagull*.
1897	Hawaii annexed by USA.	H G Wells, *The Invisible Man*.

YEAR	AGE	LIFE
1900	29–30	End of period of exile. After being held for ten days in St Petersburg, visits Krupskaya in exile in Ufa before leaving Russia.
1902	31	Publication of *What Is To Be Done?*. First visit to London.
1903	33	Attends Second Congress of Russian Social Democrat Labour Party (RSDLP). Lenin resigns from *Iskra* after the Bolshevik–Menshevik split.
1905	34–5	Attends Third Congress of RSDLP before returning to St Petersburg after Tsar Nicholas II promises a legislative assembly, the State Duma.
1907	37	Attends Fifth Congress of RSDLP in London. Takes up residence in Switzerland at the end of the year.
1909	39	Meets Inessa Armand in Paris, where he had moved to the previous year.
1912	42	Moves to Kraków in Austrian Poland.
1914	44	Arrested as a Russian spy in Austrian Poland but released after two days and leaves for Switzerland.

YEAR	HISTORY	CULTURE
1900	Second Boer War: relief of Mafeking and capture of Johannesburg and Pretoria. Boxer Rising in China.	Friedrich Nietzsche, *Ecce Homo*.
1902	Cecil Rhodes dies. Cuba gains independence from USA.	Arthur Conan Doyle, *The Hound of the Baskervilles*.
1903	King Edward VII visits Paris and French President Loubet visits London beginning of Entente Cordiale. Wright Brothers' first flight.	Jack London, *The Call of the Wild*. Film: *The Great Train Robbery*.
1905	Bloody Sunday in St Petersburg, followed by strikes throughout Russia. Russian fleet sunk in Straits of Tsushima, off Japan, in Russo-Japanese War. Mutiny on battleship *Potemkin* in Black Sea. St Petersburg Soviet formed with Trotsky as deputy leader.	E M Forster, *Where Angels Fear to Tread*.
1907	Third Duma, based on a restricted electorate, opens.	Joseph Conrad, *The Secret Agent*.
1909	USA establishes a naval base in Hawaii.	Diaghilev opens Russian ballet school.
1912	China becomes a Republic under Sun Yatsen.	Franz Kafka, *Metamorphosis*.
1914	Outbreak of First World War: Germany declares war on Russia. Russians defeated at Battles of Tannenberg and Masurian Lakes.	James Joyce, *Dubliners*. Film: Charlie Chaplin in *Making a Living*.

YEAR	AGE	LIFE
1915	45	Attends anti-war conference of socialists at Zimmerwald, Switzerland.
1916	46	Attends a second conference of socialists, at Kienthal in Switzerland.
1917	47	Arrives in St Petersburg from Switzerland and issues his *April Theses*. After Provisional Government orders his arrest, flees to Finland. Returns to St Petersburg in October before successful Bolshevik uprising.
1918	47–8	Attempt on his life in Petrograd in January and, in August, shot and wounded in Moscow.
1919	49	Enjoys a weekend holiday with his sister Anna and brother Dmitri.

YEAR	HISTORY	CULTURE
1915	First World War: Battles of Neuve Chappelle and Loos. Gallipoli campaign.	John Buchan, *The Thirty-Nine Steps.* Film: *The Birth of a Nation.*
1916	First World War. Western Front: Battles of Verdun and the Somme.	'Dada' movement produces iconoclastic 'anti-art'. Film: *Intolerance.*
1917	February Revolution: soviets established in Petrograd and Moscow. Provisional Government formed, Tsar abdicates and Trotsky arrives in Russia from New York. Attempted Bolshevik uprising in July. Civil war breaks out in Ukraine. Peace talks underway at Brest-Litovsk and armistice signed.	P G Wodehouse, *The Man With Two Left Feet.* T S Eliot, *Prufrock and Other Observations.*
1918	Treaty of Brest-Litovsk signed. Allied forces land at Murmansk; Russian capital transferred to Moscow. Formation of Red Army under Trotsky. Tsar and family executed in Yekaterinburg. End of First World War. French intervention forces land at Odessa.	Gerald Manley Hopkins, *Poems.*
1919	Rosa Luxemburg murdered in Germany and socialist uprising suppressed. Civil war spreads to Urals. Amritsar massacre by British and Gurkha troops in India.	Bauhaus movement founded by Walter Gropius. Film: *The Cabinet of Dr Caligari.*

YEAR	AGE	LIFE
1920	50	Death of Inessa Armand.
1921	51	Launches the New Economic Policy.
1922	52	Suffers his first stroke in May and a second one at the end of the year while convalescing at Gorky outside Moscow.
1923	53	Third stroke and during a short respite visits Moscow and his office in the Kremlin for the last time.
1924	53	21 Jan: Lenin dies and, against his wishes, his body is mummified for public display in Moscow.

YEAR	HISTORY	CULTURE
1920	Polish army invades Soviet territory in April but repelled in June; Red Army reaches Warsaw before turned back by Polish forces. White forces in retreat. Makhno's anarchist army smashed by the Red Army.	F Scott Fitzgerald, *This Side of Paradise.* Franz Kafka, *The Country Doctor.*
1921	Anti-Bolshevik uprising at Kronstadt suppressed.	D H Lawrence, *Women in Love.*
1922	Stalin appointed General Secretary of Bolshevik Party. Mussolini comes to power in Italy.	James Joyce, *Ulysses.*
1923	White settlers given power in Southern Rhodesia.	Jaroslav Hašek, *The Good Soldier Švejk.*
1924	Stalin out-manoeuvres Trotsky and gains power.	E M Forster, *A Passage to India.*

Further Reading

Lenin's Works

Lenin's *Collected Works* (Lawrence & Wishart, London: 1987) run to over 40 volumes and most of what he wrote is available online at *www.marxists.org*.

Essential Works of Lenin, ed. Henry M Christman (Dover Publications, New York: 1987). A useful collection that includes *What Is To be Done?*, *Imperialism* and *The State and Revolution.*

Revolution at the Gates, ed. Slavoj Žižek (Verso, London: 2004).

Lenin's writings between February and October 1917 with an introduction explaining their importance and an afterword expanding on the philosophical and political implications of Lenin's achievement.

Books

Bogdanov, Alexander, *Red Star* (Indiana University Press, Bloomington: 1984). Bogdanov's utopian science fiction novel, first published in St. Petersburg in 1908.

Budgen, Sebastian, Stathis Kouvelakis and Slavoj Žižek (eds.), *Lenin Reloaded: Towards a Politics of Truth*

(Duke University Press, Durham and London: 2007). A collection of essays that offers a fresh perspective on Lenin.

Chernyshevsky, Nikolai, *What Is To be Done?* (Cornell University Press, Ithaca: 1989). The favourite novel of Vladimir Ilyich Ulyanov offers a rare insight into the idealism and passion of Lenin.

Figes, Orlando, *A People's Tragedy: The Russian Revolution 1891–1924* (Pimlico, London: 1997). One of the more recent accounts presenting a dismally familiar portrayal of Lenin. Duplicity is discerned behind the aspirations expressed in *The State and Revolution* and its author is seen as a cunning schemer who promoted the empowerment of workers only as a tool for sustaining his wicked dictatorship as an end in itself.

Fitzpatrick, Shelia, *The Russian Revolution: 1917–1932* (Oxford University Press, Oxford: 1982). A brief but superb account of the revolution.

Hill, Christopher, *Lenin and the Russian Revolution* (English Universities Press, London: 1961). First published in 1947, Hill's style seems anachronistic at times yet it manages to convey important truths about Lenin and the revolution.

Krupskaya, Nadezhda, *Memories of Lenin* (Panther Books, London: 1970). From her first meeting with Lenin in 1893 through to 1917, Krupskaya provides a personal and very sincere account of their life together.

Liebman, Marcel, *Leninism under Lenin* (Merlin Press, London: 1980). Excellent account of Lenin's political development and the history of Bolshevism before the revolution and up to Lenin's death.

Liebman, Marcel, *The Russian Revolution* (Jonathan Cape, London: 1970). One of the best concise accounts of political events between February and October 1917, combining as it does analysis with narrative, and though it lacks the colour of Figes's book it more than compensates by illuminating the play of forces and individuals shaping the course of events.

McNeal, Robert H, *Bride of the Revolution*: *Krupskaya & Lenin* (Gollancz, London: 1973). A dry but informative account of Lenin's life partner.

Pipes, Richard, *The Russian Revolution: 1899–1919* (HarperCollins, London: 1992). This impressively scholarly and informative account of revolutionary Russia is in places a misleading guide to events. Pipes is rabidly anti-Communist, with more than one finger on the scales, and Lenin is depicted as cruel and cowardly, with a lust for power at any cost and a man whose militant politics lie buried in the depths of a virtually psychotic personality. The author was appointed to the National Security Council after Ronald Reagan became US President in 1980 so perhaps the temptation to find a similarity between Pipes' rigid dogmatism, his conviction of an absolute truth, and the Lenin of *Materialism and Empiriocriticism* is not entirely mischievous.

Read, Christopher, *Lenin* (Routledge, London: 2005). A competent and sober biography that manages to look dispassionately at the facts.

Service, Robert, *Lenin* (Pan, London: 2002). Meticulously researched and documented, this detailed and critical biography is by a noted scholar.

Trotsky, Leon, *The Young Lenin* (David and Charles, Newton Abbot: 1972). Written in the early 1930s, after Trotsky's expulsion from Russia, this is an informative account of Lenin's early years, from his childhood to his departure for the capital in 1893. The social and political background is written by an insider, someone who was there, without hostility or an agenda of his own.

Valentinov, N, *Encounters with Lenin* (Oxford University Press, Oxford: 1968). Exiled to Siberia, Valentinov escaped to Geneva in 1904 and there he met Lenin. Although they later parted company politically, these revealing memoirs of their developing friendship come across as an authentic record of Lenin's personality.

Voline, *The Unknown Revolution: 1917–1921* (Black & Red, Chicago: 1974). An insider's account of the Russian anarchist movement, its contribution to the revolution and the aftermath at Kronstadt and in the Ukraine.

Volkogonov, Dmitri, *Lenin: Life and Legacy* (HarperCollins, London: 1994). A very hostile biography by a writer who became Defence Adviser to Yeltsin following the failed coup of August 1991.

Film and Photographs

October: Ten Days That Shook the World, Sergei Eisenstein's silent film made in 1927 is available on DVD.

Films, photographs and other archive material are available at *www.marxists.org* and *www.youtube.com*

Picture Sources

The author and the publishers wish to express their thanks to the following sources of illustrative material and/or for permission to reproduce it. They will make the proper acknowledgements in future editions in the event that any omissions have occurred.

Topham Picturepoint: pp 18, 64 and 106; all other pictures private collections or public domain.

Index